430/2

The Introspective Society

The
Introspective
Society

John Barron|Mays

Sheed and Ward · London and Sydney

First published 1968
Sheed and Ward Ltd, 33 Maiden Lane, London WC2, and
Sheed and Ward Pty Ltd, 95 York Street, Sydney

Standard book number: 7220 0545 8

This book is set in 11/13 pt Times New Roman
Made and printed in Great Britain by
William Clowes and Sons Ltd, London and Beccles

Contents

Acknowledgements

Most of the chapters in this collection have previously been printed as separate articles in various periodicals. I would like to thank the editors of the following for permission to reprint articles which have appeared in their publications: *British Journal of Delinquency; Public Health; Prison Service Journal; Case Conference; Times Literary Supplement; Family Doctor; Education; Educational Research; Liverpool Daily Post; New Society;* and *The Inquirer.*

'Life itself is the laboratory in which
the social scientist must work.'

Norman Mackenzie
in *A Guide to the Social Sciences*
Weidenfeld and Nicolson
1966

Introduction

The Greeks were probably the most self-conscious people of the ancient world but even they did not develop a social science in the sense that we now know it. Much of their intuitive knowledge and inner probing went into literature and not into the empirical study of man in society.

When science did eventually come into its own in the seventeenth century its field of study was concentrated on the external universe and not on the inner nature of man and his social relationships. Physics, astronomy, mathematics made gigantic advances but still the science of man in society in the modern sense did not appear. But the eighteenth century saw the possibility of a social science brought a vital step forward in that, for the first time, men were prepared to ask what *is* before plunging further into speculation about what *ought* to be. Yet the study of social relationships continued to remain the province of the philosophers, the literati, the economists, and the historians. The necessary step of applying the notion of causality to human behaviour still required the subsequent testing of general ideas and theories by objective empirical research and this was delayed until comparatively recent years; in fact, until the very end of the nineteenth and the beginning of the twentieth century, when research based on field-work techniques and social survey methods began to develop in earnest.

In the post-Freudian world in which we now live the urge for further self-knowledge and even greater frankness has gone on apace. We have now reached a point of no return. Although the discoveries of psychoanalysis seem no longer remarkable and, indeed, are increasingly being challenged as, at most, misleading half-truths, the urge for self-knowledge has by no means abated. Sociology in more recent years, at a stride, has caught up with psychology and promises to outpace her rival. Social research in the past half-century has waxed in sophistication and greatly extended its field of application. Social psychology—an inevitable alliance between psychology and sociology— has invaded industry, penology, education, religion, and even, in recent years, sport. Rid of the encumbrance of much of its traditional philosophical adornment, sociology has become an empirical science, linking hands with the humanities and other social studies but promising in its zeal and inclusiveness to emerge in the future as the integrating and pre-eminent discipline of them all.

We live in a research-conscious age. We are learning how to ask the appropriate questions of ourselves and of our social institutions, and slowly we are developing techniques with which to begin the attempt to find the answers to our queries. In the creative arts, also, the impact of the spirit of social science is everywhere to be seen. There is a turning away from fiction towards history, social documentation, and fact: the novel is being should- ered out of the bookshops by biographies and autobiographies. The case record is replacing the literary fantasy and even the cult of science fiction is supported as much for its scientific possibilities as for its breathtaking adventures.

Nowadays the abnormal and the unusual are sometimes made the central interest of the arts. There is even a 'theatre of cruelty' in which live sufferings are witnessed. We are nothing if not exact and clinically accurate in our analysis of experience. There is no part of our lives which we do not wish to probe; religious feelings and sexual relations are now openly discussed and have become the objects of detailed social surveys. As our society becomes more open to scrutiny it grows increasingly introspective. We look in on ourselves and our social relations as thoroughly as we can because only by so doing can we hope to master our environment and solve our human problems.

This does not mean that we need to abandon moral values and ethical principles and hand over the responsibility for conducting our lives to social or any other kind of scientists. On the contrary. It means rather that obstacles which in the past have frustrated our efforts to create the 'good' society may no longer prove insuperable. Technical know-how, applied to ourselves and to our society, is constantly increasing and we can, if we so will, make use of this technical ability to serve our moral ends. Scientific knowledge, moreover, may further help by making these ends much clearer to us. Sociology is thus seen to be mainly concerned not with the formulation of values but with their viability, and with the problems that arise in attempting to implement these values in existing social structures.

Since we have now entered upon a new phase of our

development every bit as important and exciting as anything that has gone before—a phase which we may call the dawning Age of Human Science—it is tremendously important that everyone should keep in touch with what is taking place and, in non-technical language, be made conversant with the ideas and findings of social and human research. We need, as has been said, to be not only literate and numerate but also sociate. And the way to achieve this is for social scientists of all kinds to make a strenuous effort to effect communication with the wider lay community.

Social science needs popularising but not bowdlerising or cheapening in the process. This little book is, I hope, one effort in this direction. In it I have tried to cover a number of topics and issues where I think that sociologists have had useful contributions to make. No attempt has been made at comprehensiveness of scope or at inclusiveness of detail. What I have done is to present a series of essays on themes such as education or juvenile crime and to relate them to the modern family and to the pattern of urban life. I have tried to show, for instance, how planning is forced upon us, but how this very planning itself has tended to create new kinds of social injustice which challenge our skill and humanity. In a phrase, I have tried to show what the sociological view is on a number of social problems (selected solely on the basis of my own interests and research). There is no more complex plan behind the book than that.

Several of the chapters are transcripts of lectures given in public to a variety of audiences; others have been contributed to magazines and periodicals more or less *ad hoc*. This accounts for the in any case unavoidable overlapping between the various sections of the book. All, I think, exemplify an individual sociological point of view. While not every professional colleague would entirely share this viewpoint or endorse all these judgements, they are now offered between two covers in the hope that they will interest the general reader and stimulate further thought and discussion on a number of related topics which are of importance to us all.

J. B. MAYS

Part 1

The problem of race relations

1
Past imperfect and future conditional—a case study of Liverpool

The field of race relations, especially where colour differences are involved, is one where angels rightly fear to tread. One can often do so much harm by pointing to the sore spots and thus reviving the pains of subdued hostility. Yet it is mere cowardice to avoid all reference to the problem and so leave the advocates of racial exclusiveness without a moral challenge. Moreover, where there are some signs of improvement in inter-racial relations, as for example in parts of the country such as Merseyside, it is our duty to draw attention to the facts in a simple and sensible manner.

Most of us, whether white or coloured, find it hard to be completely objective on such matters as racial antagonism and discrimination. We all inherit the bad blood of the past and it is mere moonshine to suppose that the long record of the coloured man's sufferings at the hands of the dominant white man can be entirely forgotten and forgiven. Negroes still smart psychologically at the memory of their ancestors' exploitation. White christians cannot fail to be vastly uneasy when they recall the callous consciences of their spiritual forebears who grew prosperous on slavery. The situation is further aggravated by the continuing discrimination against Negroes in the United States of America, by the slightly more subtle but equally repulsive discriminatory practices in our own country, and by our only recently past imperial domination of a quarter of the world. The race riots and violence at Notting Hill and elsewhere in recent years show clearly that below the smooth surface of our civilisation there lies a boiling stew of hatred, sadism, and fear waiting its chance to erupt. It is something we must face, come to terms with, and master if the moral values we publicly espouse are to survive into the next century.

All prejudice and discrimination must be seen within the widest possible historical and psychological context. At the same time it is the task of the sociologist to point out that discrimination and prejudice spring from many sources and are not exclusively racial in origin. Human relations, both personal and social, are invariably biassed by prejudiced ideas, by notions of superiority and inferiority. Sometimes what looks on the surface to be simple racial prejudice is just as likely to be the outcome of class consciousness and social snobbery. It is important to remember, too, that the coloured populations are as class conscious and divided as the whites. Moreover, the mere possession of a dark skin does not necessarily lead to feelings of inferiority on one side nor to feelings of superiority on the other. Indians and Pakistanis, for example, have as much pride in their race and culture as any white-skinned nation in the world. Part of the complication of inter-race relations arises from the fact that many Negroes and Africans are both coloured and lower class.

Thus they are liable to experience prejudice and discrimination on both scores.

Recent legislation in this country indicates that for most of the British people the colour problem directly relates to the thorny topic of immigration. Immigration is seen by the sociologist as part of a much wider social movement which has deep roots and a long history. It is closely associated with the search that has long gone on for a higher standard of living on the part of people who perceive themselves as poorer members of the community of nations. In the same manner for many decades country dwellers have been flocking into the towns and cities and those who are conscious of having had an inferior education seek training from their more sophisticated neighbours. Obvious ethnic and physical distinctions make the competition for jobs and rewards that much more blatant and hard to conceal.

England, like the United States, has a long history of immigration. There has been a steady inflow of population for a very long time. In general the newcomers have been accepted if not actively welcomed. There is no doubt that the mixed inheritance of both countries has been greatly enriched by the gifts and labours of those who have sought their shores. There is no doubt, too, that the new arrivals have had a pretty hard time of it to establish themselves either socially or economically. Since the end of World War II the tempo of immigration has been quickening for all sorts of people, coloured and Europeans, aliens as well as members of Commonwealth countries, while the influx of the Irish is a phenomenon we have long been accustomed to accept as normal. Indeed, without Irish manual labour it is hard to see how the nineteenth century could ever have built its elaborate railway networks at such a low capital cost or how farmers would ever have gathered their harvests. The Irish came, for the most part, as seasonal workers, although several great waves of immigrants, driven by famine at home, came to Merseyside and elsewhere with the intention of settling. There has been a slow and steady process of adjustment and absorption which, over the years, has enabled most of these refugees and migrants to bed down more or less comfortably in the host society.

But what of coloured people? How have the Negroes fared? A great many came after the end of the First World War, but during the late twenties and dole-ridden thirties they were far from welcome and their presence was seen as something of an economic threat by the white native population. At a time of rising unemployment this was only to be expected. But conditions changed after 1939. Coloured colonials, and West Indians in particular, were encouraged to come over to increase our depleted man-power. Those with the necessary skills were employed in munitions factories and on other kinds of essential work. The fact that coloured men were fighting side by side with white men also made for greater tolerance and increased understanding on both sides. But, in the early days after 1945, the temper changed somewhat. Jobs were not so very plentiful that competition from 'outsiders' was appreciated. As the economic life of the country got slowly under way, much of the wartime fraternisation and sense of brother-liness was forgotten. Tensions developed as a result of competition with inevitable outbreaks of violence in various places. In Liverpool in 1949, for example, there was a short period when hostilities flared up, and white

Liverpudlians attacked coloured people in the south end on several occasions. Then, as the country recovered its economic buoyancy and jobs became more plentiful, tensions eased. Coloured immigrants moved to places with high employment where jobs were greater than the numbers of applicants. The South-East and the Midlands attracted most immigrants and seaports such as Liverpool became mere transit posts en route for more prosperous areas. Immigration from the Caribbean quickened about 1954 as openings increased in Britain and as unemployment in Jamaica and other islands soared.

It is impossible to discover what the Negro population of Liverpool is. Estimates suggest that it is something like 10,000 or 11,000, but that it is not increasing. Thirty years ago it was certainly much smaller. A social survey carried out in 1934 put the number of adult male Negroes at little more than 500.

The Negro population, although dispersed fairly widely, is nevertheless concentrated in Liverpool 8 and Liverpool 7. The majority come from West Africa, although a substantial minority are West Indians. A number of Asians, including a small group of Chinese people, who have similar but far from identical problems, tend to live in roughly the same rather dilapidated parts of the city, including Liverpool 1 and the dockland area. It is important to realise that the coloured community in Liverpool is anything but homogeneous. It is equally important to note that the Negroes are split by various significant divisions amongst themselves. Although it is a common error to lump all Negroes together and to see them as an integrated group, this is understandable. For their own part, the Negroes too seem to think of themselves as a fairly distinctive group apart from other kinds of citizens.

The Negro population is divisible into three main categories: first, the West Africans, second, the West Indians, and, third, the Liverpool-born of both groups whose families have been settled here for a considerable time. All three have characteristics which separate them from one another, with the result that their problems are very different in kind. We can put these very simply and rather crudely by saying that, culturally, the West Indians think of themselves as Europeans, the Liverpool-born think of themselves as Liverpudlians, and the Africans are much more conscious of their tribal and culturally distinct background. The psychological attitudes which spring from these different outlooks and histories make them extremely critical and suspicious of one another. These suspicions and hostilities make it virtually impossible for them to act in concert or to form a powerful pressure group working against the wider community. Those who have succeeded in establishing themselves socially and economically are embarrassed when some of their fellows react strongly against the host society. Their loyalties tend in such circumstances to conflict in the same way that individuals who have climbed socially from one class or income bracket to a higher one are often acutely embarrassed by militant trade unionism.

Social relations between members of the various sub-groups comprising the Negro community in Liverpool, then, are often characterised by a surprising degree of hostility and suspicion. Africans tend to complain about West Indians' conceit and airs of assumed superiority, while the latter, in their turn, because of their essentially

European outlook, tend to consider the Africans as backward and embarrassingly unsophisticated. The locally born are dubious of both types of immigrant, regarding them as something of an economic and cultural threat. New arrivals, the Johnny-Come-Latelies, as they often used to be called, caused embarrassment to their settled predecessors by their flamboyant behaviour and aggressiveness. The former retaliated by accusing the locally born coloureds of submitting tamely to discrimination and of being content with low standards of living and lack of proper ambition. West Indians tended to be militants and to be more obviously upset by experience of discrimination.

This division between the newcomers and the old-timers is perhaps unexpected. On purely ethnic grounds they clearly have a lot in common. But in other respects, they have much to fear from each other. Some of the newcomers claim that it is their militancy against prejudice and discrimination that has won a more equitable attitude from the host society, and that the deferential Uncle Toms would never have gained anything by their submissiveness.

The coloured community, like every other social group which has been studied, seems to divide naturally into its 'roughs' and its 'respectables'. The latter, of course, greatly outnumber the former. The former 'bad boys' and 'undesirables' who engage in illegal practices undoubtedly, however unfairly, help to get the coloured people as a whole a very bad name, and the assimilationist families naturally look upon them with more than ordinary dismay. So, too, the accentuated growth of coloured juvenile gangs a year or two ago served to bring discredit upon coloured people in general. But it is important to point out that these fights between coloured street gangs and others were invariably confined to the juvenile and adolescent age groups and were in any case not one hundred per cent racially dichotomised. Some white and near-white boys were found associated with predominantly coloured gangs and it is imperative to view such violent manifestations as much in terms of the widespread incidence of youthful unruliness as in terms of ethnic hostility as such.

Racial discrimination, however, does and can lead to outbreaks of violence. It is mere folly to deny this fact. Violence, someone once said, is the outcome of unlived life. And this is certainly true of racial clashes wherever they may occur. That such clashes are getting rare on Merseyside is true and altogether to the good. It may perhaps be that our longer experience of immigration here has taught us how to give a larger and larger share of 'lived life' to our new citizens, and that this is a lesson in tolerance that other parts of the country could usefully learn from us.

The peculiar psychological stress occasioned by their comparatively marginal status in British society makes all immigrants insecure and over-sensitive in their reactions. This is only to be expected and has nothing intrinsically to do with colour or ethnic origin. Teenagers and minors suffer from the same kind of social marginality, and react with similar annoyance to imagined slights and denigration from more favourably placed people. Teenagers, however, grow out of their adolescence. Coloured people retain the superficial signs of their difference and this means that their marginality and related insecurity are perpetuated. No wonder, then, that fresh arrivals look upon British society with mixed feelings. Nearly all want to be assimilated, to become ordinary citizens. Most suffer from discrimination either based on their ethnic difference or on their lower class background. They react by sharply protesting and also by setting up their own societies. These latter are usually of the self-help kind as safeguards against penury and acute distress. To this extent they function rather as the friendly societies did for the nine-teenth century manual worker population. But they also have another side. They tend to draw the coloured com-munity into a tight in-group, and this in turn is strongly reinforced by conflict with allegedly rejecting attitudes on the part of the white population.

The early days in Britain are bound to be somewhat confusing to those who are born and bred to the folkways of Trinidad and Lagos. And for this reason, such associa-tions as the African Social and Technical Society or embryo branches of the West Indian Society seem to have a useful role to play during the settling-in stage. They are what we have come to know in more technical language as 'transitional communities'. But there is clearly a danger of individuals and groups becoming fixated at such transi-tional stages and so never being able to pass on to the further stage of closer integration which is necessary if anything resembling final assimilation is ever to be achieved.

It is estimated that there may at any one time be some-thing like thirty of these coloured people's societies and associations in existence. Their task is to give emotional support at a time when feelings of insecurity and rejection are likely to be at their zenith, in addition to the mutual help and insurance functions already mentioned. More ambitious immigrants undoubtedly regard them as back-ward-looking and regressive, reminding them of the outgrown colonial dependency and inferiority which they rightly wish to leave behind them. But probably all immigrants need some such support if only for a limited period—just as, in dependent territories, the upper class white minority need their clubs as refuges against the strain of strangeness and implicit hostility. If they do nothing else they at least allow hard pressed immigrants to release aggression through joining in their activities and to achieve some degree of status amongst their peers. Here again there is a striking resemblance between the teenage gang and ex-colonial immigrant groups. Denied approved ways to meet their basic needs, they have recourse to spontaneously generated substitute groups to do this for them.

Not only is the traditional culture of immigrants of little use to them in their efforts to get on in British society, but it can even be a more positive hindrance. West Africans, for example, have been accustomed to a rather different male-female relationship from that which is orthodox in most British circles. It is hardly likely that their sexual needs (which have frequently been exaggerated and mythologised) are greater than those of the native whites, but they are certainly used to expressing them differently and more publicly. An African man expects a woman to be interested in him and to receive his advances as a compliment, not as an insult. His first reaction when rebuffed by a white girl is to assume that her rejection is based on colour prejudice. To some extent this may be true but it is also clearly based on the fact that such unsubtle advances violate the mores and customs which regulate inter-sexual relations in British society. If members of the host community ought to make some allowance for different cultural standards in their relations with immigrants, the latter, in their turn, must be quickly informed of the kinds of taboos and courtesies they too are obliged to adjust to if they hope to live successfully as equal members of the new community.

For these reasons, it is often suggested that would-be immigrants should undergo orientation courses before setting out for Britain. Such educational instruction could also very usefully be given on the boat coming over by duly appointed officers of the exporting country. Such advice and instruction would, one hopes, seek to explain cultural differences and similar obstacles that the immigrant is likely to encounter together with an indication of ways in which necessary adjustments can be effected. Apart from the problems of interpersonal relationships already touched on, there are similar complicated matters which must be grasped if much psychological pain is not to be experienced by the more optimistic newcomers. Many West Indians, for instance, are confused and hurt by the scepticism with which their claim to be regarded as skilled workers is met with on arrival. Both employers and unions in the United Kingdom have their own standards and regulations and these are probably much more stringent than those operative in the Caribbean islands. British organised labour is traditionally suspicious of any attempt to dilute the labour force and so weaken the bargaining power of the workers from whatsoever source the recruits may have come. Italians and Poles have encountered similar barriers and economic cold-shouldering. Again, this is another example of discriminatory practices which are far from being based solely on colour prejudice, although the sore West Indian may so misinterpret them.

The two most immediate problems which coloured and indeed most immigrants encounter are in the fields of housing and employment. The reception area in Liverpool and elsewhere has inevitably been in the poorer, older, and more over-populated parts of the city. Coloured immigrants have followed their Irish predecessors into the dilapidated districts near dockland, but unlike the Irish, who fanned out from north to south, they have been more or less confined to the southern parts of the city. In the area around the Rialto Cinema and Ballroom at the end of Princes Boulevard and Upper Parliament Street, certain of the public houses have tended to become informal community centres for coloured people, and in the tightly packed streets between the Boulevard and Park Road a high concentration of coloured families is to be found. It would be wrong, however, to think of this part of the city as a kind of coloured ghetto. For one thing coloured and white live side by side in the same flats and streets, sharing a common pattern of life and rubbing shoulders in shops and bus queues, and, for another, coloured families are sprinkled throughout the city. There are, for example, a fair number in new housing estates and places such as Kirkby, but the reception area is undoubtedly Liverpool 7 and Liverpool 8, and it is to these streets with their often large victorian houses suitable for sub-letting and conversions that all immigrants make their way. Here they obtain what accommodation they can, beginning perhaps with a single bed-sitter or even sharing with other nationals part of a house or flat.

Visiting in the Huskisson Street area on general social survey work reveals that many of the immigrants, and especially those who have brought their families over or those who have started new families since arrival, have very high standards of housekeeping indeed. One frequently finds a West Indian worker, earning good wages either in Liverpool or outside the city, living in a very well-kept and well-appointed home, the children obviously loved and cared for and a high degree of hospitality offered to even the casual caller. This is often in sharp contrast with the squalor of many of the homes of white families living in the same district, so that the oft-repeated parrot-cry 'the neighbourhood's gone down since the coloureds came' is a wicked travesty of the facts. A further illustration, indeed, of stereotyped thinking and popular scapegoating techniques.

Immigrant families are used to paying very high rents for their accommodation. Often they are fairly comfortably off and they can afford this expenditure. Indeed, less affluent white families may seize on this as a cause of grievance. Some of the wealthier immigrants have bought up old property and sub-let apartments to their fellows. There have been cases of West Indian landlords making a lot of money by such investment and after a number of fruitful years of business returning on the proceeds to their native islands to establish themselves as substantial citizens. Some real-estate firms have undoubtedly exploited the needs of immigrants to sell inferior property at very high prices to incoming landlords. The landlords have in turn been obliged to hand on the exploitative tradition to their tenants by asking for excessive rents. But there have also been cases of mutual help, of groups of immigrants clubbing together to acquire property for themselves or of landlords who do not seek to exploit their compatriots financially.

Desperate housing shortage in all the big cities to which migrants have come has inevitably led to hardship. While the civic authorities in London or Birmingham, Liverpool or Leeds, face the future with an ever increasing rate of dilapidation and an ever increasing demand for accommodation, the general plight of immigrants is bound to be tough. And, what is equally obvious, people who have lived in the cities longer are bound to feel aggrieved if they see newcomers gaining more points than themselves on the city housing lists. Thus when cases are discovered of up to six immigrants living in a single room and paying rents of thirty shillings each, the facts have to be interpreted in the light of general overall shortage rather than in terms of the rack-renting of unscrupulous landlords battening on helpless people's miseries.

The competition for scarce accommodation is undeniably aggravated by the operation of a colour bar. An analysis of landladies in London made some ten years or more ago showed that approximately 70% were unwilling to accept coloured students as lodgers, and, as far as very dark Africans or West Indians were concerned, the proportion of refusers was nearer 85%. The veto on coloured lodgers also extends to those who want to buy or rent accommodation in select areas whose residents are concerned that they shall not go down socially.

Discrimination is always a depressing fact of life, springing, as it does, from that pattern of superiority-inferiority relations which so far have characterised all civilised societies of any size. But, even so, there are grounds for hope for the future. Improvements are taking place, however slowly. Time is, in fact, on the side of toleration, sympathy, and dignified human reciprocity between people of good will. In cities such as Birmingham, for example, after initial resistance of a strong nature was expressed when coloured immigrants arrived there, it has been shown that after residents got to know the new arrivals as courteous and unaggressive public servants in, for example, the role of bus conductors, much of the original prejudice evaporated in the less 'classy' areas at any rate. Similarly, Myrdal, the famous American sociologist who has made a lifetime's study of race relations, stated in his classic *The American Dilemma* that well over three-quarters of his informants favoured segregation in housing facilities. But Merton, another well-known American sociologist, has suggested that this evaluation was altogether too sweeping. He points out that there is a marked difference in the attitudes towards coloured people between whites who have had experience of bi-racial neighbourhoods and those who have not. The latter are always more prejudiced and frightened of admitting coloured people as their neighbours. But those who have already had this experience are much more egalitarian in outlook and less hostile to the idea of living in racially mixed neighbourhoods. In a community he studied and called Hilltown, he discovered that three times the number of people who were inexperienced expressed hostility towards the idea of bi-racialism as compared with those who had had the experience hitherto. Moreover, when after a while a further enquiry was made, it was found that an interesting change of attitude had occurred on the part of the prejudiced inexperienced residents whose responses now were much more closely akin to those who had had experience of bi-racialism before coming to live in Hill-town.

This kind of slow adjustment process is clearly operative whenever coloured immigrants and native whites find themselves willy-nilly brought into close association. A recent study made in Nottingham and published in *New Society* stresses the fact that social integration—at least in the work situation—is much more successful there than most people might *a priori* have supposed. In a number of Nottingham firms it seems that personal relationship has led to a natural diminution of racial prejudice. It did not seem to follow, however, that good relationships at the work level necessarily made housing and social contact any the easier. Clearly housing presents an especially acute problem. There seem to be two main factors associated with housing, both of which make it unlikely that any very substantial improvement in the general situation is likely to take place during the course of the next few years. The first of these is the fact of chronic shortage of accommodation for all lower status and lower income groups in all our big cities, making competition and jealousy inevitable. There is only one way to improve this situation and that is to build sufficient accommodation for all the people who require it. In Liverpool, particularly, this rebuilding is taking place so slowly that it will be very many years before the slums have been cleared and replaced by new property. Moreover, by the time we have caught up with the backlog of decayed buildings, ones which were previously adjudged habitable will not any longer be so. Housing is indeed Liverpool's major public problem, causing untold misery to thousands of people and making life often quite intolerably frustrating. Although the white and coloured people suffer from this chronic shortage, there is little doubt that coloured people suffer disproportionately to their numbers, and will for a very long time indeed tend to be regarded as outsiders and treated with hostility.

The second main factor is socio-economic. Streets into which immigrants move tend to become depressed and devalued. The social tone falls and, at the same time, those residents who think of themselves as 'nice', 'respectable', and so on, begin to move out. For this reason they are on the *qui vive* for the first sign of coloured tenants, and it is more than a landlady dare do to admit even a coloured university student into residence. It is simple enough for those who live in better-class suburbs to condemn such an attitude, but we have to remember that the devaluation of property is perceived as a serious economic threat. The position of the property owners in a street 'threatened' by the arrival of coloured residents is almost identical with that of the superior group of detached middle-class houses on the rural fringe who suddenly find that the local authority's decision to erect a new housing estate for ex-slum dwellers in the fields opposite has at a blow knocked £1,000 or more off the value of their property. The fact that, in the case of the inner urban street, the economic threat is to some extent imaginary, and that, as a matter of fact, prices of houses and rents could rise with the arrival of a wave of eminently exploitable immigrants should not really surprise any of us who are at all familiar with the strange ways in which human psychology works—for instance, in waves of panic on the stock exchange. It is a fact that people are rarely completely rational. We are all tremendously swayed by our emotions and these, in turn, can be vastly moved by purely social and snobbish influences.

At the work level, as has already been suggested, there are indications that inter-racial hostilities are lessening somewhat. Experience in the Midlands and in the London area, where there is still full employment, will not be strictly comparable with experiences on Merseyside, which has one of the largest unemployment problems in the whole country. But even here, as far as one can judge, competition over jobs is much less severe than it was twenty years ago. But even though the actual business of getting some kind of work may not present too serious difficulties, there is the associated problem of the migrant who is aggrieved because he cannot find a job comparable at the levels of skill and status or at a wage that he considers appropriate. The man who hopes to be accepted as a craftsman all too often finds that his earlier training is deficient by British standards, and transfer in the white collar field of employment seems to be even more tricky than in manual and technical work. The experience of being economically and technically degraded often leads to the familiar 'chip on the shoulder' mentality resulting from the immigrant's conviction that the reason for his down-grading is yet another flagrant instance of discrimination based on colour prejudice.

British trade unions have never quite made up their minds about their proper attitude towards colonials and other immigrants. While the operation of a colour bar is officially contrary to the philosophy of the Labour movement, there have been cases of unofficial attempts being made to get employers to agree to a limit on the numbers of coloured workers being employed. But the situation is extremely fluid, and wide variations of attitude are to be found between region and region, and even between branches and shops in the same industry. At the employment, as at the social and housing, levels, the host society is painfully divided between acceptance and rejection, incurably ambivalent and torn between what is morally right and what is economically advantageous.

The fact that other parts of the country are more prosperous and offer more work than Liverpool has meant that this city has no very severe or immediate immigrant problems. Colour clashes, at the adult level at any rate, are not likely to recur unless there is widespread economic depression. But while the Midlands and the South-East are siphoning off that proportion of immigrants permitted to enter the country under the existing legislation, the situation in Liverpool is likely to remain stable and possibly to improve. The problem is thus resolving itself not so much into an immigrant problem as into the question of racial integration. It is, in fact, largely the problem that other parts of the country will be obliged to face in the future, when many of those ex-colonials have decided to settle down and become British citizens. With fewer newcomers and fewer temporary and transient immigrants to cope with, Liverpool is confronted by a very minor version of the social and human problem that still afflicts the United States of America.

The question is basically a moral and philosophical one. Its ultimate solution will be achieved only by the exertion of strong moral pressure on every individual citizen reinforced by whatever legislation and public control is considered necessary. Time alone will not bring about the ultimate solution of what is basically a problem of human commitment to a policy of genuine equality and democratic justice. It is a much wider question than how white and coloured can get on together amicably and live side by side peaceably. For the coloured minority are but examples of socially disadvantaged and socially depressed people everywhere. They are the helpless victims of our chronic and inveterate tendency to stratify our social relationships hierarchically and to maintain wide status distinctions and differential financial rewards between different occupational groups.

The experience of the locally born coloured families, then, may be taken as indicative of the present situation in Liverpool and as a measure of the tasks that await future action. Very little research has been done on this topic and relevant publications are few and far between. Members of the University Department of Social Science about ten years ago followed up a limited number of households which had one or more coloured parent to see how they were faring and what difficulties they were encountering. A brief report on this material* appeared in the *Sociological Review* in 1960. Some of the main findings of this research suggest that experience of discrimination, though common, is not universal, nor quite so crippling as might have been supposed. About a third of the families with whom contact was made felt that they were troubled by racial prejudice. These families were found amongst the lower class but also comprised some of those whose heads were more skilled than others, who maintained a fairly

* by I. H. Maddox

22

high standard of behaviour and of child care. They also tended to be those with somewhat 'lighter' skins. White wives of Negro husbands tended to suffer socially for having married across the colour line, and there were distressing cases of women who, as a result, had been rejected and ostracised by their own kinsfolk. Such mothers inevitably feel embittered towards their white relatives and cannot help bringing up their own half-caste children in an atmosphere of suspiciousness and sensitivity to prejudice. We can see in this way how hostility is generated and maintained over the years, how people who have been hurt become hypersensitised to insult, and, by so doing, expose themselves to further real and imagined contumely. The consequences of racial prejudice are cumulative and self-perpetuating.

However, those coloured families most hostile to white people were those who lived in the coloured quarter. Families which were poor or which had unskilled or unemployed heads were often acutely resentful. But it is important to note that by no means all who had experienced racial prejudice were bitter about the experience. Some of the more highly educated, who were striving to improve their social standing and had moved away from the coloured quarter, accepted a degree of discrimination as inevitable.

Three main family types were observed. (a) Assimilationist families, about 29%, who were seeking ultimate absorption into the city community. They accepted the cultural goals and behaviour norms of respectable British society. In the main they sought accommodation outside the coloured quarter and dissociated themselves from their racial fellows. The fact that the father was often born and bred in Liverpool seemed to help the process of assimilation to a considerable extent. (b) Intermediate families, some 55%, who had come to accept the fact that they lived in a more or less segregated community but who had accommodated themselves to the superior white society and, as a cause or consequence of this state of mind, were found to be, on the whole, rather apathetic and defeatist. (c) Families comprising the remainder of the group studied which were positively hostile towards white society, sensitive to discrimination and active in protest. They frequently took refuge from anxiety by trying to reject the cultural goals of the host community and looked nostalgically back to their own homelands. This was a comparatively small group, comprising only 16% of those whose reactions were assessed. By and large, the majority accepted a position of social inferiority and had come to terms with it in the same way that other under-privileged people feel themselves obliged to do, many, perhaps, even accepting society's verdict on them as soundly based.

A rough index of discrimination is the extent to which coloured families have friends across the colour line and the degree to which they do not experience serious difficulties in getting employment in competitive circumstances. It is the general impression of social workers and teachers that the children of coloured or racially mixed parents do not experience much discrimination during their early years. Some research evidence in schools reinforces this impression. It is not in fact until adolescence that colour becomes a serious handicap. While attending local schools or youth clubs coloured children make many friends and are frequently elected as captains or as senior boys and girls. It is not until the school leavers apply for jobs that they are brought up against the hidden colour barriers in British society. Girls seem to have better job prospects than boys but both have a somewhat restricted choice of occupation. But it is clear that there are more coloured lads in skilled employment than there used to be and that this is a result of a general economic improvement. Professional careers are practically closed to girls. Nursing is probably the only professional work they are freely admitted to, and this, no doubt, because of the dearth of recruits in hospitals. A fair proportion of coloured boys are unemployed and as the competition for school leavers builds up this is likely to continue to be the case. Girls can generally find work of some kind. Boys, in the main, have to be content with semi-skilled or unskilled work. All are handicapped by a restricted range of occupation. Coloured girls seem to find it extremely difficult to get jobs as shop assistants or as secretaries or office workers. Personnel officers when questioned would say defensively: 'Of course the firm has no colour bar, but the customers would object', or, sometimes, even, 'We would take them on but other girls would refuse to work alongside them'.

It is generally recognised that some firms engage staff without any reference to colour while others will not. Nevertheless, no employers have been found who openly admit to racial discrimination. There is always the general category of 'unsuitability' to shelter their prejudice behind.

In the past many coloured boys went away to sea or joined the armed services. These still seem to be popular careers but fewer and fewer openings are available, partly because recruitment is generally tighter and calls more and more for special competence. It is a fact that the proportion of male Negroes in unskilled manual work is greater than for the local labour force as a whole and is probably nearer 50% than 30%. Their career prospects are, then, far from being open and many men are obviously ashamed of the nature of the work they have to accept. Furthermore, chances of promotion to supervisory grades are slender. The recent study of West Indians in Nottingham by Bayliss and Coates confirms this finding. Although they found no evidence that any friction at work level existed between the West Indians and others, and that on the contrary a good deal of mutual respect had been built up, chances of promotion were much poorer for the immigrants. The same kind of bias seems to operate also in jobs which involve handling the public with any degree of real authority. It will be a severe test for our racial impartiality when coloured police constables or even traffic wardens are appointed. The time when this test occurs may not be so very far away, however.*

The onset of adolescence ushers in the dawn of disillusionment for the local born coloured. The sporadic sparring between white and coloured juvenile gangs in south Liverpool has hinted at arbitrary hostility. So too have the off-the-cuff comments in street or playground, cries of 'bloody nigger' and so on, been picked up by the children from their offensive parents and echoed in moments of anger and provocation. But it is not until schooldays are over and the youngsters try to establish themselves alongside their peers that the full force of their social disadvantage strikes home. The sphere of personal relations turns out to be almost as trying as getting a job. After spending their childhood alongside white boys in

*One or two such appointments have now (June 1968) been made.

the classroom, coloured girls find themselves less sought after by either white or coloured boys than white girls. Coloured boys seem to find it easier to find white girls willing to partner them, but coloured girls on the whole have to be satisfied with coloured husbands. There are powerful social traditions and biasses underlying this attitude to coloured women, who are thus obliged to undergo this unfair double discrimination.

There are, of course, exceptions to all such generalisations. Many Negroes have white friends and cronies. Families which are most assimilated have most white friends, and it is only a very small group of poorly adjusted newcomers who have all their social and personal relations within their own ethnic group. Nevertheless, the rate of assimilation is sluggish. Few church communities have active Negro members. In a recent study in London, Clifford Hill claims that 94% of those West Indian immigrants who used to attend churches at home have stopped doing so on arrival in this country. One of the reasons for this falling away, he thinks, is the patronising attitude of their fellow christians which can in the end make them even more self-conscious than acts and words of open prejudice.

The business of helping both local-born and immigrant coloured people is hence a tricky psychological matter. There must be no over-doing the helping hand and it is equally undesirable to leave such disadvantaged groups severely alone. Help of a sympathetic and enabling character must be offered. This has meant in Liverpool, in addition to the normal social services which function for all, the setting-up of one or two institutions specifically aimed at helping the coloured community, at least with their short-term problems. One of these, Stanley House, a community centre in a large building in the Liverpool 8 area, has now been in existence for over twenty years. In its time it has sought to cater for both adult and juvenile groups with varying success. Although fairly early on in its history it professed a policy of running activities for 'coloured people and their friends', experience has shown that this is a much more difficult task than was supposed. Far from creating a neutral area for inter-racial and cross-cultural association, such as the British Council centres offer, it has tended to emphasise coloured hegemony and to build up in-group sentiments. In so far as this has happened, it must be taken to be working against the long-term interests of coloured citizens by putting some-thing of a brake on assimilationist aspirations and achievements. But, in the short term, it may well have fulfilled a useful function by offering socially handicapped people opportunities for fellowship and social activities otherwise hard to come by. I was myself Warden of Liverpool University Settlement during one period when the organisers of Stanley House made a deliberate effort to recruit boys who were members of our Settlement clubs for their own coloured organisation. I can well recall the strains of conflicting loyalties that this policy generated amongst youngsters whose families had enjoyed a long and happy association with the Settlement. It seemed to me then, and it still so appears, that this kind of policy, by emphasising divisions, is not in the ultimate interests either of coloured families or of the local neighbourhood considered as a living community.

The idea of Stanley House as a social centre fostering

racial and cultural integration is by no means denied by the foregoing comments. If, in the future, its policy of attracting white members and white groups under its roof succeeds, it may well prove to be a valuable instrument for promoting social change in desirable directions. Emphasis on coloured people as such, however, as opposed to residents in the locality, will have to be greatly modified, if not eliminated, if such an outcome is to occur.

The services of an Overseas Welfare Officer, sponsored jointly by the Liverpool Personal Service Society and the City Council, with initial help from the Colonial Office, is another institution which the city has set up with the primary object of helping coloured citizens with their varied problems. The Overseas Welfare Officer has now been working as a joint PSS and Corporation venture since 1953. In the early days the Welfare Officer was established in a room at the Settlement in Nile Street, but subsequently he was transferred to Stanley Street in the centre of the city. He has been called upon to give help and advice in innumerable ways and on all kinds of problems. It may well be that the success of this experiment could be usefully emulated by other cities, such as Bristol and Leeds, which are facing the kinds of social and personal problems in relation to coloured immigrants and residents which Liverpool experienced at a much earlier date.

What of the future? How much has the experience of Liverpool to teach the country as a whole? What are the chances of finally resolving these vexing questions of racial prejudice and discrimination?

The recent restrictions on the number of immigrants will undoubtedly help by reducing the possibility of having increasing reservoirs of unemployed coloured people. But restriction is not likely to result in the early or satisfactory solution of the long-term problem of assimilation and absorption. It may indeed foster further inter-racial suspicion and hostility.

The prospects for those families who have left or who are eager to leave the coloured quarter of the city and who have a strong assimilationist drive are undoubtedly good. As their mode of life approximates more and more closely to the middle-class standards which compose the acceptable social norms, as more and more intermarriage takes place and colour becomes less and less an observable distinction, the integration of such families seems to be assured. There will be difficulties and trials ahead of them but in time the ultimate objective will surely be attained. But the prospects of the locally born coloured people who cling to the relative security and familiarity of Liverpool 7 and 8 are by no means so good. There is a danger that, at the lower end of social scale, the prospects for integration are in fact not improving but deteriorating. Those families who feel deeply insecure and draw closer to their ethnic group for support could in the end produce something akin to a ghetto mentality and a ghetto organisation. In London, for instance, there are signs that the Negro group is becoming self-contained, providing its own amenities, shops, and services for itself as a distinctive unit. Similarly in Liverpool there are established coloured clubs and groups, shops and cafés. A further malign influence is the fact that socially and economically inferior coloured families are obliged to live in an area which is notoriously the centre of Liverpool's seamier night life, and that some of the dubious clubs and vice rings are associated with the wilder and more delinquent immigrant elements. Popular prejudice against these things can so easily rebound on to the heads of the well-behaved and respectable coloured families, who stand, it must be remembered, at the base of the social ladder, handicapped by lack of skill, by poor educational attainments, and by their colour. We have already in this country created a lower class proletarian group of underprivileged people. It may happen that below this group there will be a further underprivileged class composed entirely of coloured people who, stripped of their own leadership potential, will form something like a depressed caste condemned to permanent inferiority as hewers of wood and drawers of water for the wider community.

Indeed, it is hard to see how this is to be avoided. Obviously slum clearance schemes, rehousing projects and better educational provision will together ease the problem. The discreet work of the Overseas Welfare Officer and the sympathetic help of civic officials and employment advisors will also be invaluable. But the ultimate problem is, as always, a moral one. It concerns the nature of our democratic institutions themselves. It is basically the question of how we are to treat all underprivileged people, whatever their racial or cultural origins. How we are, in fact, to apportion the rewards of a prosperous and technologically advancing society equitably and justly for all—what social justice in fact comprises. It is impossible to take a very optimistic view of the future as far as this social problem is concerned. It is difficult to believe that, in a phrase, social justice and Utopia are around the corner. But we must strive with all available resources to bring this desired state of affairs a step nearer to fulfilment every month and every year.

Not until suburbia exhibits the generosity and hospitality of the slum will immigrants, and coloured immigrants especially, feel anything like at home in this island.

Part 2

Urbanisation, the family, and social change

2
The social problems of urbanisation

I imagine that we would all agree with the comment that today we find ourselves living in a rapidly shrinking world. The ever-increasing speed of travel and of communication methods is simply forcing us to come closer together, whether we like it or not. At the same time, virtually throughout the world there is a steady and inexorable drive towards the creation of a common urban and industrial culture. The pastoral way of life is dying; in the not too distant future it will be merely archaic for vast areas of the world's surface and for the great majority of people.

These facts are obvious enough, but what are not always quite so clear are their social and political consequences. We are, in fact, living at a time of profound and rapid changes which in many parts of the world involve a complete social revolution. But we are all bound up with this process. All that separates us is the rate of change and the position we have reached along the general line of development. To discuss the problems of modern society is more or less to discuss the problems which arise from the operation of the main trends to which we are all, to varying degrees, exposed: that is to say, the problems which arise from urbanisation, from industrialisation, from bureaucratisation (which must inevitably come into being in societies committed to rational policies and decisions) from the growth of mass media and of rapid geographical and cultural communications. Thus to discuss the problem areas of the world as a whole is to some extent to examine the same kinds of problems at differing stages of growth in different countries and societies. If what I am saying is true, if we are indeed moving towards a common way of life, then we are all facing a set of common problems which tends to make the whole world kin. And the solutions to these common problems will not be individually determined, but in the last analysis will only be found to be soluble in terms of the creation of general consensus about means and ends, followed by the appropriate communal action. This can be seen most clearly perhaps in relation to the general danger of war. An outbreak of hostilities in any part of the globe is a potential threat to us all. So, too, in the field of economics I believe that prosperity in any country will be seen to be more and more dependent upon the absence of poverty elsewhere.

Such gigantic problems as face us today demand a concerted and concentrated approach by all experts to assist the common people of all lands to understand the nature of the social world they live in and so be in a better position to act responsibly and creatively towards it. This, I take it, is the central purpose of this conference and of the international conference which it foreshadows[1].

[1] This chapter was originally delivered as a lecture before an invited audience in Coventry convened by the Bishop to discuss the general topic of urbanisation. The conference was convened to initiate a series of world-wide discussions ultimately

What has the sociologist as such to say about these issues of urbanisation, industrialisation, bureaucratisation, and mass communication which is specifically sociological and may be deemed to be in any way helpful to other specialists or, above all, to his fellow citizens? One thing is clear: the problems of modern city life are the focus of many other scientists' and thinkers' attention. Architects, engineers, planners, physicians, psychiatrists, economists, geographers, administrators, politicians, and many other specialists have each got their part to play. The sociologist may hope that his contribution will be complementary to the work that these others are doing. His specific approach may in broad terms be called holistic and humanitarian. By 'holistic' I simply mean that he attempts to integrate a variety of approaches in such a way that he can produce a synthetic overview and so be in a better position to suggest possible solutions to whatever problems arise. In this chapter we will be more narrowly concerned with the phenomenon of urbanisation, though the other forces and trends which are shaping modern society cannot be ignored entirely even when we concentrate on any single aspect of our social experience. One thing, at least, is abundantly clear. We cannot reverse the secular trend. We have no choice but to come to terms with city life, with increasing technological development and with the rapidly extending automation of labour, whatever our misgivings may be. It is a simple matter of fact that all over the world men are coming closer and closer together into vast cities and conurbations. This is truly the age of Megalopolis, as

---

culminating in an international conference in Coventry in 1968, the year of the diocese's golden jubilee.

Lewis Mumford called it, of the ghost city of paper which has grown up alongside the modern 'insenate' industrial town. Mumford really didn't like cities. He felt a great urge to clean them up, to humanise their environment, and many of us will be sympathetic to his point of view without going all the way with him in every criticism that he made in his well-known book, *The Culture of Cities*[2].

Like most other developments, urbanism is a challenge. It presents points of progress and of danger. It is a challenge that must be faced and mastered if our civilisation is to go on. Sociologists, therefore, will not be of much use to their fellow citizens if they merely stand aside on the touchlines, observing the process, analysing it but offering no advice. If the man who has made the diagnosis cannot produce any kind of prophylactic, it is pertinent, perhaps, to ask who can.

The general problem can, it seems to me, be approached under four main heads: (a) physical, (b) psychological, (c) moral, (d) social. While we will largely concern ourselves with (b), (c), and (d), it is important not to ignore (a). All four aspects need to be kept constantly in mind in attempting to come to terms with modern urban life. They overlap and are interdependent. Moreover, all are closely related to, and dependent on, economic factors, about which I propose to say nothing, merely observing, as William Temple did, that the spiritual cannot flourish unless its material and physical base is soundly secured, for the psalms will not feed empty bellies nor will the Lord's Prayer heal the sick.

Furthermore, there are four or possibly five different

[2] Secker and Warburg, London (1938).

kinds of urban areas which need to be considered. These are down-town and suburban and old and new. We have the older poorer inner-city localities and the fairly well established suburbs on the one hand, and the new housing estates and redeveloped parts of the old inner slums on the other. Then there are the New Towns which have been springing up so dramatically and hopefully in the past twenty or so years, which present rather different and special problems.

The end we seek is the creation of a truly healthy habitat for human living. We want to achieve an environment within which all men's potentialities will be enabled to develop to their maximum extent and where individuals will uniquely count and be cared for by the community as a whole.

There is so much to be said on all this that I am obliged to be selective. I want to try to confine my remarks to a few aspects of the main topic which have a special interest to social scientists and with regard to which we may have something useful to say. First, and perhaps most important of all, is the theme of 'community' of which so much has been written and of which, also, so much remains to be said and attempted in practice. This concept of community is in many ways the key to all that I want to say to you this evening. It is a sociological and also a moral and spiritual idea. It is moreover especially relevant for christians, for the christian church, it seems to me, is first and foremost to be thought of as a living and abiding community of persons. The word *community* implies social relationships of a particular kind. Necessarily it also involves extensive group action underpinned by a sense of corporate responsibility. Before a true community can be said to exist a number of people have to share certain important aspects of life together, and for this reason the notion is invariably linked with communal residence of a fairly well-defined geographical area. Men, being social by nature, always tend to establish relationships. The question of paramount interest in this connection for town planners is: Ought they deliberately to set out to foster interaction between people or should they merely let events take their own course? Should they, that is to say, just make up a plan of roads, dwellings, shops, and so on, and leave it to chance or to the residents themselves to make their own contacts? Or, on the other hand, should they try to shape the physical environment and plan the layout in such a way that it will *ipso facto* enable the maximum amount of interaction to take place?

Answers to these questions vary, depending almost entirely upon the differing viewpoints of the experts. They can only be decided, in the last analysis, by making value judgements about the desirability or otherwise of neighbourly contact. But what sort of contacts and how frequent ought interactions to be? Individual preferences apart, are there any objective grounds for saying that, in rebuilding our towns and developing our cities, we ought to seek consciously to promote neighbourliness and foster local group solidarity?

There are several reasons which some social scientists would advance which support the idea that such questions as we have asked should be answered affirmatively. Perhaps the most cogent is one that relates to the mental health of the inhabitants. If there is any evidence, for example, which suggests that some kinds of physical evironment tend to produce mental ill-health, ought we not then, if this is so, to plan in such a way that people are not exposed to their possibly deleterious influence? As a matter of general social policy, ought we not to prevent this kind of problem from arising in the first place?

If we turn to the psychiatric and sociological findings in this field we will be faced with divergent evidence. The psychiatric data are rather more conflicting than the sociological data. We will have to do our best with what is available and not seek impatiently for certainty in such areas where fact and value, objectivity and subjectivity, are almost inextricably interwoven. In any case, social science does not pretend to deal in certainties, only in probabilities; social scientists have not got the answers to all the problems men ask even at the social level; they can, however, offer suggestions and provide perspectives. But in the final analysis personal judgements must prevail. The hope of the social scientist is that his work will enable personal judgements to be more informed and sophisticated than they otherwise might be.

Studies of what is taking place in the new out-county residential estates are usually regarded as the touchstone for deciding whether or not there is a significant connection between people's mental health and where they are obliged to live. The new estates catering for overspill families from older, down-town city localities can be taken as being experimentally crucial in this regard. Until quite recently it was believed that the mental health of the new estate dwellers deteriorated as a result of the move. Compared with their lives in the older neighbourhoods from which they had come, it was claimed that the lives of families living in the new estates were socially impoverished to a dangerous degree: they were often cut off from their relatives and kinsfolk; they had to spend a lot of time and extra money in travelling to and fro, both for work and for recreation; above all, it was believed that the new areas lacked the variety of social amenities and organisations necessary for the maintenance of a satisfactory relationship with other residents of the locality. This produced symptoms which were sometimes called 'New Town Blues' and 'Suburban Neurosis'.

However, a fairly recent study made by E. H. Hare and G. K. Shaw of the Mawdsley Hospital, London[3], of two populations in the Croydon area, one central and the other a new estate, seems to indicate that no great differences can be found in the mental health of the two lots of residents, and that what small differences can be detected are probably more attributable to such factors as family size and poor physical health than to any absence of social amenity or similar feature of the new environment. One may also wonder how many of the new estate dwellers, who do get mentally depressed and develop symptoms of psychiatric disturbance, might not have done likewise even had they not been moved and simply allowed to remain where they were. There is, of course, no possible way to answer such a question, but Hare and Shaw's enquiry does suggest that in any population there will tend to be a proportion of people prone to both physical and mental ill-health.

Sociological studies show a similar inconclusiveness. The well-known Bethnal Green enquiry, *Family and*

[3] *Mental Health on a New Housing Estate*, Oxford University Press (1965).

Kinship in East London[4], maintains, in contrast to Hare and Shaw's findings, that residents of the new districts do feel themselves isolated, that they become lonely and are consequently unhappy. Housewives, they claim, are especially vulnerable in this respect since they are the most cut off from their familiar roots, from frequent contact with their parents, relatives, and former friends, and obliged to busy themselves in their homes for the best part of the day. Their husbands, by contrast, do get away to work, often returning to the district they have left, where they can meet old cronies and kinsfolk. Moreover, while at work they tend to have adequate interaction with other people and so need fewer social contacts in their home area. John Mogey[5], on the other hand, who studied families which migrated from inner Oxford to a new suburban estate, suggests that the people there, at any rate, are much more sociable in their new environment than they were in their former one. Mogey found, for instance, that in the new locality, although meetings with kindred diminished, friendly relations with neighbours sharply increased, and, although church attendance dropped away, membership of clubs and similar associations increased considerably. In other words, the changed way of life brought both losses and gains which may indeed on balance more or less have cancelled each other out.

Moreover, research undertaken by my own university's Department of Social Science in the Merseyside area tends to suggest that the friendliness of some old inner city residential neighbourhoods can be over-estimated, and

[4] By Michael Young and Peter Willmott, London, Institute of Community Studies and Routledge and Kegan Paul (1957); Penguin edition (1962).

[5] *Family and Neighbourhood*, Oxford (1956).

that there are dangers in generalising from extreme examples of either type[6]. Neither the snug tightly-knit urban community nor the freezingly lonely suburb are invariably to be expected, and, as more and more community studies are made, a much more balanced average picture of city life will no doubt emerge.

Much, in fact, seems to depend on the composition and qualities of the different populations. For example, we found that people in general were rather more sociable in the new township of Kirkby in south-west Lancashire than they were in some parts of the dilapidated victorian heart of the city from which many of the families had migrated [7]. I can clearly remember calling on occupants of single flats and bed-sitters, during the course of the field-work for the survey, who felt themselves to be so cut off from their neighbours that one of their greatest anxieties was that one day they would fall ill and nobody would know or miss them, and that, as a consequence, they might be left unattended for hours, even days on end, before any kind of help should arrive. I also recall in this connection a story told to me by an American friend. She was living at one time in an apartment in a tall block of flats in New York and had been in residence for several years. On the day the removal men came to take her belongings to a new address she met her immediate apartment neighbour for the very first time. 'Gee,' the neighbour said to my friend, 'I'm so sorry to see you're leaving. You've been such a good neighbour to have.' Which being interpreted

[6] Vereker, Mays, Gittus, and Broady, *Urban Redevelopment and Social Change*, Liverpool University Press (1961).

[7] N. Rankin, 'Social Adjustment in a North-West New Town', *Sociological Review*, vol. II, no. 3 (1963).

means, I suppose, that the good neighbour is nowadays one who minds his or her own business, keeps to himself, never obtrudes, makes no demands and no noise. I am sure you will all be familiar, too, with the terrible story of the New York girl, Catherine Genovese, who in March 1964 was killed within sight and sound of her own apartments, where thirty-eight local residents not only failed to go to her help when she screamed but also refrained from calling up the police. How far, one may bitterly ask, can good neighbourliness go?

If we return again to the more scientific survey evidence, it seems true to say that social and human problems are as frequently to be found in old slum districts as they are in the new estates. The isolation and fragmentation of what have been called the 'twilight zones' or areas in transition of big cities attract, if indeed they do not also help to create, some distinct kinds of mentally ill people—for example, schizophrenics, retreatist drug addicts, sexual deviants, and similarly marginal types. The very anonymity of these rooming-house districts seems to have a special appeal for this kind of individual. The police of every big city could point to such shady districts, but we must not confuse them with the more usual kind of lower class inner urban neighbourhood as described by Young and Willmott and others. We must distinguish between low status and socially disorganised districts, between Bethnal Green and a red light district. The old neighbourhoods such as Bethnal Green or Ancoats in Manchester may have been characterised by strong social bonds and firm neighbourly ties, but, since the physical fabric was worn out and inadequate, the authorities had no alternative but to begin rebuilding them and so, in effect, changed much of their former character. Thus, as a matter of general policy, we were obliged to sacrifice slowly achieved homogeneity of outlook and stability of securely anchored family and community life, to obtain a physically adequate and healthy environment for the residents of over-populated areas. The hope is that, in the end, with the process of time new bonds of fellowship will develop in both old, rebuilt, and out-county localities, and thus that the general social loss may turn out to be only temporary. Such indeed is the message of Hilda Jennings' fascinating book about the people of Barton Hill in old Bristol[8]. 'If we turn back to the history of the old area', she wrote, 'we find that it went through similar phases of change. In its early days there was the same severance from familiar places and kinship ties . . .', yet out of it all, when the new residents got firmly settled into their locality, there finally 'emerged a society in which individuals counted and the social bond was strong'. In other words, it takes time to make a community. A community is a living thing. It must grow slowly according to its nature. It cannot be produced overnight by the stroke of a pen or the decision of a committee. And also, alas, like other living things, it can so easily be killed.

It seems clear that today changes are being forced upon us whether we like them or not. Progress at certain levels and growing economic and technical means, the spread of new ideas and aspirations, and a firmer understanding of such older ideas as social justice and equality are impelling us ineluctably forward. The task of the planners, aided by the social scientists, is seen, then, to involve the acceptance

[8] *Societies in the Making*, Routledge and Kegan Paul (1962).

of change but an endeavour, also, so to arrange things that the minimum of social dislocation occurs, and, at the same time, trying to make sure that policy decisions will be of such a nature that they will be likely to foster the maintenance and rebirth of firmly based family and community life. The family is, as you know, a remarkably tough institution—rather like the human heart physiologically speaking—and an enormously resilient one, capable of surviving all manner of changes and vicissitudes. A desire for married family life is as strong a tendency today as it ever was in the past, and this in the face of many fears and lamentations expressed by social critics convinced of a general decline of public values and private ethical standards. Most married couples, too, seem to desire to have children, and this brings us to one of the most important aspects of urban planning. Children, like the aged, have very special needs. They must, for instance, be safeguarded against the ever increasing tide of road traffic and against other physical dangers.

We need to give much more thought to this problem and, in this country at least, to be much more imaginative and experimental in our thinking. The main need outside the home is for children to have a safe and interesting place in which to play, not too far away from their own front doors, where they can enjoy some of the traditional recreations and games and, under sympathetic adult guidance, have a go at novel activities. It is not solely a question of physical safety and wholesome amusement. There is, also, to an unknown degree, the association between idleness, boredom, excess free time, and various kinds of juvenile delinquency, of which vandalism and violence against property is perhaps the most obvious. Children need opportunities to experiment and even to have adventures in an environment which is reasonably controlled. Adventure and junk type playgrounds have been experimented with somewhat sporadically by a handful of enthusiasts but, in this country, are still looked at somewhat askance. Hybrid of the strip-cartoon and the junkyard, these imaginative play provisions, because of their messiness and noise, may offend local residents and disquiet adult visitors. All too often the needs of the young are sacrificed to the convenience of the older members of the community. Their needs, moreover, are often completely misunderstood, as though grown ups have quite forgotten what it was like to be a child.

The ideas behind the adventure playground movement are, as one writer has so well said, 'as old as history, as fundamental as childhood itself'. To build, to construct, to improvise, to put up and pull down are primitive activities which appeal to any normal child. 'It is only when these natural inclinations are thwarted by an industrial civilisation that adults have to think up alternatives' and to try to recreate the conditions which make this sort of creativity possible. The urban child is cut off from all natural life, from growth of plant and tree, from water, stream or river, from sand on the seashore. Not surprisingly when he does get into the country he thinks of birds as targets for catapults and trees as things to be hacked down for firewood. If he finds crabs in a rockpool it will not be long before he is stoning them to death. The urban child is psychologically disorientated, cut off from man's natural roots, seldom called upon to battle with the elements or to learn to co-operate with nature. This is a deep sickness which no playground movement can as yet hope to cure. But it can make a beginning, and the beginning is to teach and assist the child to use his hands and imagination in coping with whatever simple materials he finds, to allow him the satisfaction of putting one stone upon another, of placing a few planks together to form a hut, of digging a hole, or lighting a fire in the open air. In some places re-education can go one stage further, encouraging contact with living growing things, by establishing a garden which the children can help to plan and where they can experience the great satisfaction of planting a seedling and watching it grow and come into flower[9].

Part of the task of the social planners, then, is to produce a comparatively safe yet stimulating and deeply satisfying environment in which children's games and play needs are given parity with other basic human requirements—not merely relegated to the margins of life to be provided, if resources become available, at the end of a very long queue.

I have spent rather a long time on this topic of children's play because it is often overlooked, but of course facilities for positive recreation for youngsters in cities is only one consideration amongst many. What, we may ask, are the proper functions of the other public institutions in building up strong community sentiments? Amongst the most important of existing institutions, all of which have a bearing on how and when people interact socially, are the school, the church, the local community centre, the voluntary club, and—by no means the least important—the shopping, entertainment, and eating and drinking facilities. Most families have children, and this means that most families in a given locality will at some time of their existence be brought into active relationship with the local schools, possibly too with the available youth service organisations. A great many people will meet in

[9] J. B. Mays, *Adventure in Play; The Story of the Rathbone Street Adventure Playground*, Liverpool Council of Social Service (1957), 5.

the shops, pubs, cafés, coffee bars, sports grounds, bingo halls, dance halls, parks, and so on as and when they are provided. The degree to which such communal facilities are available or not must have a strong influence in determining whether local residents get an opportunity to meet and do things with their neighours, and, to this extent at any rate, they may be thought of as the necessary foundation for community life. Not everyone goes to church or similar worshipping community, although Sunday schools are rather more actively supported, but the very presence of a church or chapel and the occasional calls from priests and ministers—above all, perhaps, the physical sight of a church in a neighbourhood where weddings and funerals are seen to take place—helps to give an area some focal points and to sustain, however weakly, the idea that deep down we all belong to one community and have some mutual obligations to each other. The sense of community is thus often very fragmented, manifested and evidenced in subtle ways in addition to the more self-conscious community organisations that may exist in an area. Such influences and institutions are to my mind much more important than some of the other things to which planners and architects seem to give their attention: neatness of design, aesthetic pleasure in layout, and open space which often fails to be functional at any level.

In the process of this exposition it seems that I have more or less answered my own general question about the desirability or otherwise of social policies aimed to promote and encourage a sense of community. In my view the design and fabric of new estates or redeveloped neighbourhoods not only should not discourage social interaction, they should seek positively to encourage it. At the same time, one must put in a caveat that those who simply don't want to involve themselves in social relationships of an organised kind should be able to opt out. Sociability should not be produced by undue pressure on individuals to join this, that, or the other group. We don't want a neighbourhood organised as a kind of Big Brother's Holiday At Home. But I think that we must plan for the majority who want to do things together, rather than for the minority who prefer solitude. Freedom of choice must, however, be safeguarded and proper privacy for individuals and for single families must be respected. At the same time we need to see to it that no one should be lonely who hungers for companionship, and that those who are solitary in their activities are solitary from choice, and not simply because the neighbourhood has failed to provide them with the opportunity of meeting and doing things with other similarly placed people.

What we all want to know for the purpose of making future plans is whether this thesis is broadly speaking the correct one. One of the ways in which we can find this out is by carrying out more and more community studies centring round these topics so that we can, in the end, cover something like a genuine cross-section of the country's population. This is a task that local residents' groups might well find very interesting and profitable. If they could enlist the help and co-operation of social scientists in undertaking this kind of self-study, a widely scattered and truly representative body of knowledge, based on adequate fieldwork carried out in many different kinds of community (differing in size, geographical location, ethnic composition, degree of industrial development, extent of urbanisation, and including, of course, European and non-European experience) might in time be built up.

There is one related topic of extreme importance which must be touched on, however briefly, in a paper purporting to discuss the social problems of urbanisation. That is the problem of how, if at all, we can hope to achieve and maintain a mixed community. By 'mixed community' I mean societies which could be both representative of different social class and income groups and which are also multiracial. These are very different things, but the two often overlap in the poorer parts of big cities, which are also usually the zone to which immigrants, in their early days, are obliged to make their way.

The question we have to ask ourselves very seriously indeed is whether we want to work and plan for mixed communities, or whether on the whole we think it more advisable to cater for different ethnic and occupational groups in different types of neighbourhoods in distinct parts of the town. Sociological evidence suggests that homogeneous communities are much easier to organise than mixed ones, and that racial and class ghettoes serve to reduce inter-group tensions, and so assist the maintenance of an equable *status quo*. If, however, we decide on moral, religious, and/or political grounds that we don't want to perpetuate and deepen social and other divisions, what practical steps can be taken to break down barriers in an urban industrial society? Any evidence on this issue would be of very great interest to us all, and if case studies can be made by local people of successful mixed communities working and living together amicably and constructively they would be of prime importance not only to social scientists but to the world.

I should have thought myself that it would be sheer folly to start off *ab initio* either with entirely homogeneous communities or with highly mixed populations made up of a great variety of different groups. The study of Hilda Jennings in Bristol which I have already referred to seems to indicate that we should begin with a fairly composite population and gradually and deliberately try to make it more mixed and less monolithic over the years; possibly by feeding in families with backgrounds somewhat superior in the social sense to those of the existing inhabitants of the area, but not so far removed as to provoke hostility and resentment from either side. At the same time as slightly 'superior' groups are introduced, educational and community organisations would presumably be striving to modify the general mode of living more in the direction of what, for want of a better term, we may call a middle-of-the-road way of life and its associated values and standards.

Social justice, it seems to me, demands that we should not acquiesce in the existence of residual slums any more than we should remain content with middle and professional class suburbs as permanent features of the social structure. The direction and the pace of induced social changes being brought about via the planning and redevelopment of our cities are political issues which will have to be honestly faced not tomorrow but immediately.

This brings me to my third and last major topic: the political condition of the local community, and more particularly the relationship between national and local government. Little space remains to say much on this

53

important subject, but it is in some ways, I think, the key to the way in which urbanisation develops in the future and to an understanding of what this will increasingly mean for the quality of social life and social relationships within any community.

In the past thirty years or so we have seen a trend towards centralisation of government, and sundry functions which used to be the prerogative of district authorities have been transferred to county authorities. There has been a similar trend for central departments to take over from all kinds of local committees. The process which has thrown up the idea of regionalism and regional planning and of national planning for the country as a whole is entirely rational. There is so much to be said for it in the way of efficiency and equality that one day we may find that we have travelled too far in the direction of centralisation. That the dangers are not imaginary and unimportant is witnessed to by a similar concern of government during the same period to try to bolster up the powers of local authorities wherever possible, as for example placing on them more responsibility for the more humane services of health, education, and welfare.

A second factor which has a bearing on this issue is the tendency for local and regional authorities to rely increasingly upon the services of professional experts, e.g. planners and architects. Often these professionals are socially mobile, lack any sort of local patriotism, and owe as much allegiance to their own professional colleagues and associations as to their employers. Finally, public indifference, ignorance, and apathy can result in the professional administrators having too much power in decision making, with the result that local government becomes something of a farce, or is the stamping ground for individuals who do not represent the majority view. This is, I believe, one of the most insidious threats that democracy in our time has to face; apathy from within, and the associated idea that those who take an active part in public affairs are merely busybodies, cranks, timeservers, and men on the make.

In conclusion, may I say that it seems to me clear that there can be no healthy community life without a keen participation and interest in either parochial or national affairs. Present day tendencies towards a withdrawal of the family into its own snug domestic shell must react adversely both upon local government and upon the quality of personal relationships within an area. Calls to community service will go unanswered, the isolated will become more lonely, the frustrated more depressed and ill. Problems related to grassroots democratic responsibility are also closely connected with the whole business of mutual aid. Where will we find the leaders which every town and little locality needs to get things done? In the past we have often imported superior social class individuals to provide leadership thought to be lacking in the neighbourhood itself. This was most obvious in the field of social work and in education. Is there another untapped source in the area itself, or must we continue to rely upon imported professionals? And, if we do, will this not depress the interest of local people even further and drive them into an apathetic or hostile 'them and us' mentality? We simply don't know enough about this kind of vital issue, and the need for further research in this area is a matter of urgency. Here again, local residents' groups might find a topic to concern themselves with.

Community building in my view is not outmoded or irrelevant to modern conditions: at both humane and political levels it is still an urgent necessity. A woman returned voluntarily to her old slum house in a dingy back street because, as she complained to the local school-teacher, 'Do you know, Sister, you couldn't even borrow a pan up there!' Some people would say that this is a trivial issue. I have heard sociologists cry out with impatience at the idea that this is even worth talking about. Of course, borrowing a pan is trivial in one sense, but for this woman it was symbolic; the pan represented a pattern of relationships in which she felt happy and at home. We don't want people, I imagine, to return to insanitary property or to repopulate the slums. For that matter we don't particularly want to facilitate the borrowing of pans. But the concept of a community, the idea of a neighbourhood, the feeling of mutual obligation and brotherly concern for one another's problems and affairs are surely worth preserving. Moreover, if we don't consciously try to preserve and develop them, they will atrophy. For the first time perhaps in the planet's history some societies have the technical skill and the economic strength to shape their own environment and mould their own community as a result. What is often lacking is the moral vision, the imaginative passion and ethical compulsion to bring this about.

Basically, the problems of urbanisation in modern industrial society are, as I said at the beginning, the problems that part of the world now faces and that the whole world will have to face tomorrow. It is worth while pausing at this point in our history to try to see what we can learn from the attempts so far made to achieve the solution of our urban problems in the hope that the communities of tomorrow will profit from our mistakes and build accordingly.

'The art of city planning', said Henry S. Churchill, the American social scientist, 'is four-dimensional: consisting of length, breadth, height, and imagination.' The greatest of these is imagination, but only imagination disciplined by sound sociological knowledge and informed with a humble desire to love and serve our fellow citizens.

3
Urban family and social life

In the preceding chapter we took a general and widely ranging look at some of the social and psychological problems associated with the increase in urbanisation. In this chapter, and in the two chapters which follow it, we will try to examine in greater detail some of the topics which have already been raised. In particular we will pay special attention to what is taking place in down-town neighbourhoods and in new suburban areas because these seem to be acutely sensitive to social changes and it is here more than anywhere else that the stresses and strains of modern urban living will be most keenly felt.

It was inevitable that social research would in its early days closely adhere to the line of interest laid down by the nature of social work and the bias of social workers. It was not only 'problem-centred' (for it will surely always seek to find answers to significant questions!), it was positively pathological in its absorption with the themes of poverty, destitution, neglect, and crime.

One of the things that must be admitted is the general paucity of information about the everyday life of ordinary urban families. For this reason, the survey carried out in Bethnal Green by Michael Young and Peter Wilmott[1] is particularly valuable both for the information concerning the lives and attitudes of East Londoners which they have made available and for the stimulus to similar urban studies which their book afforded.

There is a stereotype of the deviant individual and of the problem family which presupposes an equally clear concept of normality and conformity which may be very far from the truth. What seems to be required, therefore, in the development of social research on the community side is a series of studies of the ways in which ordinary folk pass their lives and of the sorts of satisfactions they are able to derive from their work and their recreations, from their social and their family life. Such investigations are not likely to commend themselves to everyone since they are by nature undramatic, and, in the final writing up, may prove to be a trifle pedestrian and even frankly boring. Nevertheless, they are of first class importance both to the academic sociologist concerned with the analysis of social systems and for the social worker attempting to cope with problems of adjustment and maladjustment. There are indications that such broad studies of social and family life in relation both to planning and to group behaviour are likely to become more numerous. The studies of communities in Liverpool and Sheffield[2] are examples of this developing interest, as, too, are the attempts made in recent years to relate both crime and delinquency to the

[1] *Family and Kinship in East London*, London, Routledge and Kegan Paul (1957).

[2] *Neighbourhood and Community*, Liverpool University Press (1954).

59

social patterns of particular areas[3], emphasising the essential normality of such behaviour as opposed to the earlier and more pathological interpretations.

In this article an attempt will be made to discuss certain aspects of the social life of inner Liverpool which were revealed during the course of a survey carried out by the Department of Social Science specifically related, in its earlier stages, to housing conditions and problems of redevelopment, which has been given the general title of 'Crown Street' after the major roadway that almost bisects the area, and also by a number of scattered studies made by members of the staff of the University Settlement in the south dockland region of the city.

One of the first things which emerges from the Crown Street investigation is the lack of uniformity within the localities in which the studies were executed. This in itself is perhaps not very unexpected; nevertheless, it disposes of some of the facile generalisations concerning the people and the modes of living of inner urban areas which planners and administrators may be tempted to form and to make use of in preparing their development schemes.

Travelling the extent of the few hundred acres in the survey area involves passing from one more or less distinct type of community to another in many respects its complete opposite, although for the purposes of the Registrar General's census statistics both would be grouped together and by the casual observer might equally be described as working-class or as low status localities. On such a walk one would pass from the city's multi-racial rooming-house district with its comparatively highly mobile population to

[3] *The Social Background of Delinquency*, University of Nottingham (unpublished report), 1954.

the solid respectability of families living in bye-law terraces where many were the owner-occupiers and had resided there for several generations.

Massive generalisations are clearly out of place and must be replaced by a careful examination of specific parts of the wider areas so that due weight may be given to differing patterns of life, attitudes, needs and values both in the preparation of redevelopment plans and in the development of theories of urban culture. People are more various, and the inhabitants of contiguous geographical sections are more diverse than we would like to believe.

Since the inner city areas are not homogeneous either in their physical environment or in their social structure and cultural traditions, talk about neighbourhood or community is therefore somewhat misleading. What appears to exist is a series of small homogeneous clusters or fragments of broken, or of potential, communities, located within short distances of each other, and often evidencing markedly divergent social habits and standards. The 'black' and the 'white' streets of 'Radby', the midland town studied by the Nottingham University investigators, indicate a comparable dissimilarity of behaviour within an area populated by people of roughly the same income group existing in practically adjacent streets.

The research workers engaged on the Crown Street survey for instance found that they were obliged to break down the whole area in subsectors which, during the progress of the enquiries, were seen to possess both physical and social characteristics distinguishing them from one another. In particular, very marked social differences were discovered between part of one ward immediately adjacent to the city commercial centre and part of another ward

61

further inland, which were in many respects in striking contrast to one another[4].

Meanwhile something may be said about Crown Street as a whole and of the principal findings derived from the questionnaires, administered to a sample of five hundred and fifty households out of a population of about 45,000, which have a broad and general relevance. The area is largely residential in character, with a mere sprinkle of light industry. The majority of the residents inhabit single-family houses, although in one ward there are many multi-household dwellings and lodging houses in what were formerly merchants' and wealthy businessmen's mansions. The population is predominantly working class though there are a few professional people in one locality, and the majority are engaged in purely manual employment. About 60% of all employed residents are engaged either in dockland or in the commercial centre of the city.

The population of the whole survey area turned out to be rather more stable, in the geographical sense, than had been supposed, although certain parts, notably the rooming-house district, were functioning as a reception area for immigrants from overseas and as a zone of transition through which families often passed en route to better residential areas. 'Flittings' were also by no means uncommon in this latter area.

Half of all the heads of interviewed households had lived in the area for ten years, and many had lived there for much longer periods, and had in fact been born and bred there. Only about a quarter of all the heads of households, whether male of female, had travelled far during

[4] See 'Cultural Conformity in Urban Areas', *Sociological Review* (July 1958), for a more detailed account of such differences.

their lifetime from their birthplace addresses, which were located either in Crown Street itself or in the immediately neighbouring city wards. Relatively to the inner Merseyside zone, the Crown Street district could be characterised as stable, although a fair number of people who once lived there have now moved either to the new housing estates or to better-class districts further from the river.

The urban family, so far as could be ascertained during the preliminary investigations, reveals a tendency to approximate to the conventional middle-class nuclear pattern of father, mother and children living together in one household, as distinct from the old, multi-generational slum household of former days, which might have included both grandparents and grandchildren living under the same roof.

Questions asked regarding frequency of contact between members of the kinship group, assessed for this purpose by mutual visiting once or more during the previous month, revealed the fact that there were very few families which were not in close touch with kinsfolk. While there was a minority who had brothers and sisters living fairly close by with whom they were not in regular contact, only 1% of the heads of households had married children living nearby with whom they were out of touch. Moreover, a very high proportion of all heads of households, 40%, made their first homes on marriage with one or other of the spouses' parents. There was a strongly marked tendency for them to settle with or near to the parents of the wife as opposed to the husband's. This matrilocal trend has also been noted in studies made in Bethnal Green and in the St Ebbe's[5] district of Oxford, and is probably

[5] *Family and Neighbourhood*, Oxford University Press (1956).

63

characteristic of working-class life. The reasons for this are obvious enough. It is the women's task to look after the home and to bring up the children and the newly married housewife would naturally wish to be as near as possible to her own mother in the early days of her marriage for the benefit of the advice and practical help she would thereby receive. Moreover, in general it seems true to say, that it is the womenfolk who take the initiative in binding the kinship group together and in promoting exchanges of visits and other forms of social contact. Once the woman goes, the ties and claims of intimate family association tend to fall away and become less important.

All accounts of urban living discuss the concept of neighbourliness. For the Crown Street study this was interpreted in reference to the people that the householders said they would turn to in times of stress and sickness. It was abundantly clear that the majority of Crown Street residents relied upon their relatives for assistance at such times rather than upon neighbours or friends. Sixty-six per cent of those who answered this question affirmed that they would turn to their own kith and kin, while only 12% said they would have to rely upon neighbours and a mere 6% to others, which included friends and the voluntary social services.

In many cases of course this implied nothing more than members of the household staying off work to look after one another, but in a sufficient number of instances it involved receiving help from relatives living elsewhere, sometimes quite a long distance away. Four per cent of those questioned admitted that they had nobody to whom they could expect to turn in times of trouble, and they, without a doubt, represent a potential problem group of rootless and often sick people, lost amid the restless multitude of the vast and lonely city.

It was not found that the presence or absence of relatives had any positive correlation with people's expressed desire to remove from or to remain in a particular locality. Desire to move appeared to be conditioned almost entirely by the needs of the single generation family, the parents showing themselves to be more concerned with their children's welfare than with the maintenance of close kinship ties as such. There is reason to believe that this held true more for those younger married heads with young children who wished to leave the area than those who wished to be rehoused locally. Evidence obtained from thirty-three families in the dockland community near the University settlement who had been rehoused locally in one new block of corporation flats suggests very strongly that many of the families in such flats not only have a closely knit kinship system but, further, that this pattern supplies the main network for help and borrowing. Many of those questioned in the Settlement neighbourhood, moreover, stated that they chose the particular locality mainly *because of the presence of relatives* living nearby.

Thus, while it may be true that the function of the kin-group is in general tending to become less important a feature of urban life, there is no reason to believe that it will ever atrophy and die out. Cyril Smith[6], in his survey conducted with housewives of Dulwich, has convincingly illustrated the important contribution that the family and the neighbourhood group can and still do make to the solution of many types of social problems in spite of the immense growth of the public social services of the Welfare

[6] *People in Need*, London, Allen and Unwin (1957).

State. The kin-group, as has been shown, in an inner urban area like Crown Street is still regarded as the source of additional help and support in time of trouble. Parents and children are seen to be locked together by particularly strong and enduring bonds even though relationships with inlaws, with aunts and uncles, cousins and the other members of the extended family circle, are wearing thinner.

Our general evidence on this important topic is somewhat inadequate but it would probably be fair to say that those who are socially ambitious either for their children or for the whole family wish to leave the inner areas entirely irrespective of ties of kinship existing, while those who are less ambitious socially and who for many reasons prefer to live in these inner wards, value highly, amongst other things, the support and companionship that the presence of kinsfolk ensures.

One very surprising finding of the Crown Street survey was that relating to members of the various households' participation in what could be called organised social activities including adult education as opposed to recreation obtained through purely commercial channels or by regular attendance at particular pubs. Only 9% of those with children under school age had any who were members of youth organisations. The adolescents showed an even lesser degree of participation in organised leisure time groups. Only 2% of those households with adolescents had any who were members of recognised youth groups. A very small minority of households had any members over the age of eighteen attending recognised recreative activities, the vast majority of all ages apparently finding all the social intercourse they desired either in street associations or in informal contacts in local shops, dance halls and pubs. It is difficult to know why this is so and whether or not this dearth of attendance at organised activities is a result of the lack of such organisations in the inner Liverpool area or a consequence of the people's own lack of enthusiasm and a support for such ventures. At least one youth club was known to have been established by one of the neighbourhood churches, only for the youngsters who attended it to smash up the furniture and behave in so aggressive and uncooperative a manner as to force its closure.

However, there was found to be a statistically significant correlation between the length of time a family had been resident in the area and the extent of its various members' participation in organised leisure groups. The longer households has resided in the locality the more likely were their individual members to be active members of such organisations, which suggests the hypothesis that association with what social institutions exist in such areas may be taken as a fair indication of a family's general social integration. It seems reasonable to believe that people who do not succeed in establishing relationships with their neighbours are likely to be the social misfits and to be, or become, the social problem group.

The figures for church attendance and contact with a worshipping community turned out to be much higher than might have been expected for an area whose organised group activities were discovered to be particularly slight. A substantial number of heads of households stated that they attended religious services regularly; some households had children attending Sunday schools and some, although not regular members of a particular church, were fairly frequently visited either by the clergy or lay workers.

Altogether 45% of the households in the survey were church attenders or members while a further 21%, though non-attenders, said they were visited by clergy or parochial representatives. One elderly lady spoke warmly of the work of the Sisters of Mercy in her district. 'They visit old ladies and bed-ridden people, if they're on their own, and bring a hot dinner and make up the bed. They were good to me when I was ill. They don't mind whether you're a catholic or protestant. If there's no one else, they'll step in.'

The importance of such experiences can hardly be exaggerated and may make all the difference between well-being and despair to some of the old, the sick and the lonely who are left to their own devices amid the isolation of a great city.

While contact with the various churches was one of the positive factors exerting an integrative and healing influence on the area generally, it was apparent that education, both in its formal and informal aspects, played no great part in the lives of the people. There is reason to believe that only a small minority of parents are very keen for their children to obtain either a grammar or a technical school education. Only a few asked for their children to receive homework and, by comparison with more suburban neighbourhoods, the schools experienced very little pressure from parents with regard to their children's possible performance at the 11-plus examination. The influence of group opinion in promoting this negative attitude towards education and to the benefits it confers was brought out by one mother, who, during an interview, said that her son had deliberately failed the 'recall exam' for a possible technical school place because he was afraid that 'the other boys in the street would laugh at him if he won it'.

For the vast majority of children Crown Street like dockland offers a one-way education system. Out of the sample of over five hundred households only two boys were at that time (1956) attending grammar schools and two more boys were at technical schools. The position regarding girls was slightly more favourable; eight were in full-time attendance at grammar schools but none were at technical schools. A little less than 3% of the whole school-age population of the area, then, were attending selective schools, a small fraction of the children who in better-class districts enjoy this privilege.*

The picture of educational disadvantage is further exemplified in the fact that comparatively few Crown Street householders have young people serving apprenticeships or undertaking any sort of training for skilled work. Amongst the sample households only twenty-seven young people between the ages of fifteen and twenty-one were found to be engaged in anything that could be described as an apprenticeship, bound or otherwise; and of this number the vast majority, twenty-six, were boys.

There emerges, then, a general picture of an intellectual desert in the older, residential centre of the city, which is similar in many of its characteristics to the communities of dockland. Very few families value education; an even smaller number of parents are willing to make sacrifices to improve their children's chances of rising via the educational ladder; most people are content with unskilled employment and, in this respect, it is clear that the teenagers are following in the parental pattern; there are some indications of group hostility to school and to all

*The numbers have, of course, risen during the last decade, but in comparison with the better-off areas the disparity remains.

learning; parents even feel embarrassed at being asked to attend a concert in which their own children are appearing simply because it is taking place at the Philharmonic Hall where they would feel 'out of it'; only a small minority of children, young people or adults attend any form of organised recreation.

On the physical side, the general decay and deterioration is matched by the cramping inadequacy of many of the old school buildings (although, in fairness, it must be admitted that the two new RC schools are both elegant and spacious). Moreover, there is little intercommunication between school and home. The teachers live well away from the locality and only two schools, out of the eight primary and secondary modern schools within the Crown Street boundaries, have parent-teacher associations.

Richard Hoggart[7] and others have drawn attention to such facts in other parts of our great industrialised communities which suggest that there are 'dead-patch' zones or sub-cultures where the 'bandwagon mentality' is positively anti-educational to such an extent that it is no exaggeration to say that there is a real danger that we are 'moving towards a kind of new caste system, one at least as firm as the old!' In former days it was the barriers of social class and economic disadvantage which held enterprising families and able children in thrall. Today, as a result of the 1944 Education Act, many if not all such handicaps have been removed. But still in these older, blighted areas the hoped for transformation has not taken place. The average child seems to be culturally chained down. He is surrounded by an adult world where most of the

[7] *The Uses of Literacy*, London, Chatto and Windus (1957); Penguin edition, 1958.

workers have jobs which are 'not intrinsically interesting, which encourage no sense of personal value, of being a maker.' Work is for money and money is for enjoyment. Enjoyment for the most part means entertainment of the passive sort, much of it absorbed visually and uncritically in a 'sexational', 'candy floss,' 'juke box' world provided by commercial mass amusement syndicates.

Those who as teachers or social workers have to work in such sub-standard areas are often moved to complete despair. So much of their effort seems to be in vain: they are battling against forces which are too strong for them and which they do not understand. All they know is that the district where they perform their daily toil is a long, long way from the biotechnic dreams of Lewis Mumford[8] and from its fundamental of 'a child at work in a stable and reassuring world: a pair of lovers at play in a room where the scent of lilacs may creep through the window, or the shrill piping of crickets be heard in the garden below.'

What, practically speaking, can be done to ameliorate or alter the general culture of such areas to bring them more into line with British culture as a whole and to prevent waste and frustration recurring?

There is, of course, no simple answer to this question. It is only possible to put forward a number of suggestions, which may promote social changes in the direction we desire and bring about a gradual revolution of ideas and attitudes. I would myself pin most hope on sensible replanning schemes and a development of existing educational services, making full use of the statutory powers for further education and youth services. The usual objection to the provision of any further services or new institutions is that

[8] *The Culture of Cities*, London, Secker and Warburg (1938).

71

they are excessively costly for the community to afford at the present time. The answer to this objection is that the resources already in being, both financial and human, are probably sufficient for the job; that what we require is not an overall increase of services but a concentration and a redeployment of them so that they will be operative where the need is greatest. At the present time, we are so obsessed with ideas of parity that we endeavour to extend what may by some be termed the 'marginal' social services to cover the entire community, irrespective of individual or group needs.

The case for zoning special areas for a system of high priority services in the centres of our great industrial and commercial cities seems unanswerable. What is lacking is the imagination and the administrative initiative to undertake such a zoning scheme. Once the decision has been taken it should be possible for all the resources of social work, education, and planning to unite in a concerted effort to remould the physical, social and institutional life of the 'dead-patch' areas. This is, after all, what is happening in the new towns and on the new housing estates everywhere up and down the country with results which are, on the whole, and judged over one or more generations, satisfactory. The task of redeveloping the inner residential areas of our cities has received much less thought and attention.

Much could be achieved by a policy of gingering up the schools in these sub-standard areas, by giving them all the help and equipment they need and by encouraging the keenest and most able teachers to apply for posts on their staffs. Positive efforts could also be made to forge a link between school and home. A revitalisation of, say, the school welfare and attendance department could undertake (what is surely a crying need) attempts to get families functioning better both in terms of their personal relationships and in terms of budgeting and organisation. Each school in such an area might have its trained welfare officer, entrusted with the task of linking teacher and parent, able to co-operate with and to bring in assistance from every other social welfare worker and agency. And then there is the youth service, which has seldom been given the support it deserves. Immense things have been and still could be achieved through youth organisations if only we would take them more seriously and support them more imaginatively.

The general need is, in a phrase, to plan for a more viable community in the down-town districts. This would involve on the planning side a resolute drive for clean air in the establishment and extension of smokeless zones to cover the residential as well as the commercial parts of the inner urban areas; a lowering of the population densities wherever possible; a discontinuation of the policy of building more multi-storey flats, or of any blocks over three or four storeys as the maximum; a better use of land and open spaces so that much of the present wastage of land resulting from excessively wide verges and parapets, etc. could be used for proper playgrounds and (especially valuable in city areas) for adventure type playgrounds under trained leadership. On the social side a more viable community would involve a determined effort to link home and school more closely, and to associate parents and social workers and teachers together in common enterprises concerned with their children's welfare and, in addition to a development of parent-teacher associations, experiments with smaller neighbourhood groups such as street committees might be started to assist, for example, in raising funds or giving other help to local youth or old people's clubs.

Advances could be made on all fronts simultaneously and to a co-ordinated plan, bearing in mind at the same time the need for continuing research in all aspects of such community undertakings. At the present time very little indeed is being done in the older residential centres of our great commercial cities apart from the erection of new dwellings, shops, and flats. Like the new housing estates these inner urban areas are all too often vast deserts, deserts of bricks and mortar, concrete and steel for which no single civic department and no one group of officials has an overall responsibility. Hence, the present state of affairs to which Richard Hoggart and others have drawn our attention. The problem of such districts is not one of social pathology. The residents as a whole are not unduly delinquent, deviant or sick, although a substantial minority are. It is simply that in the existing conditions the majority, both young and old, are condemned to live in an environment which is seriously lacking in those facilities and stimuli which could give them fuller, happier, healthier and more socially valuable lives. To rectify such a state of things is surely a matter of urgent social justice.

Note: Since this chapter was originally published the Plowden Committee Report has made similar recommendations, especially regarding a policy of positive discrimination in favour of down-town primary schools and the need for much closer links between school and home. These recommendations, however, have yet to be implemented, and, as usual, finance is the major problem.

4
Moats won't help: community planning and human values

One of the major social problems that faces us during the next few years is how we are going to prevent town planning and redevelopment schemes driving deeper and deeper wedges between us. Social workers are becoming increasingly conscious of the fact that one of the unexpected and highly undesirable consequences of the redevelopment of big cities is the tendency to encourage new class distinctions. The sheep and the goats are being separated out more certainly and irrevocably than at any time in our history. As the more able and ambitious people move away from the older neighbourhoods under slum clearance projects, those who remain behind usually comprise a 'lower caste' of less talented and less favoured folk. At the same time, many of those who fail to 'make a go' of the demanding life of the new housing estate filter back to the city and seek to resume their former mode of living in the old district.

Before 1939, the poorer parts of London, Glasgow, Manchester, Newcastle, and the other major cities contained many very capable and intelligent people who were at that time prevented from achieving their ambitions by social forces over which they had no control. Many of these now famous old neighbourhoods possessed both character and charm. The people who lived there seemed to have roots and a sense of community often lacking elsewhere. The Ancoats district of Manchester typifies the friendly atmosphere of former times, when the human spirit seemed to be able to overcome economic and physical disadvantages so magnificently that visitors from all walks of life forgathered at its University Settlement and were greatly impressed by the cooperative and welcoming attitudes of the local residents.

Today, as a result of the many changes that have taken place in the general framework of our society, those older neighbourhoods often seem to be much more depressing places than ever before. Despite the fact that, physically, many are obviously in much better shape, the quality of life does seem to have deteriorated. The word *slum* (one of the most horrible yet most graphic terms to be thrown up by colloquial speech) used mainly to refer to living conditions. Nowadays it can also be used to describe an attitude of mind. The squalid courts and narrow streets have increasingly been replaced by sturdy modern buildings, yet the social stigma, the unholy halo of a bad reputation, often remains.

And in those blighted districts which have not yet been rebuilt, such as the Cable Street area of Stepney, the taint of a bad social reputation is stronger than ever.

One deplorable result of this branding of localities is that the inhabitants know exactly what other people think about them and the more sensitive and more ambitious are correspondingly more keen than ever to get away. Thus the less favoured districts are increasingly abandoned and shunned by so-called 'respectable' people. It is a tendency which, if unchecked, will once again result in the existence of 'two nations' and two cultures facing one another with fear and misunderstanding as rich and poor did in victorian times. And if that happens, so much the worse for both modern democracy and the christian way of life.

This evil can only be avoided by deliberate policy and control on truly democratic lines. What we have got to do is to eliminate both physical and cultural slums. Through sound planning and reorganisation schemes we have got to demonstrate that we love our neighbours, not depress them further. We must help and not condemn, and, above all, we must not acquiesce in their acceptance of their own alleged inferiority. We have got to rebuild our great cities and conurbations from the foundation upwards, not merely improve the suburbs; the whole way of life of the *less favoured* neighbourhoods must be raised to the national average. This demands a long-term and imaginative plan to make the city centres and the old adjacent residential neighbourhoods, not only tolerable but desirable places to live in. And not desirable and attractive for one income group or one social class, but for a complete cross-section of the community. We must learn how to make city life so attractive that people will regard it as a privilege to live there.

In the past there have been many objections to building high blocks in the city centres, a necessity forced on the planners by high rateable values and scarcity of sites. Objections to flat life, however, may not be so much a dislike of the idea of having a high-level home as a criticism of the kind of accommodation which in the past was generally associated with low social status. Life in city flats, however, could possess its own peculiar charm and beauty as the City of Westminster estate at Pimlico illustrates, or some of the later inner district schemes of Birmingham, where lawns and blossoming trees and an existing lake have been incorporated in satisfying high-storey layouts. But probably one of the best examples of what imaginative planning can offer is the new civic centre of war-ravaged Coventry which combines amenity, safety, and aesthetic satisfactions in an altogether original and thrilling conception. At Coventry, it is clear, planners have realised the idea of the city as a way of living in its own right.

Not only must the physical plan for rebuilt urban centres seek to combine utility with beauty, it must also make for genuine physical and mental health. In this connection the drive for clean air demands more substantial support. The provision of more 'smokeless zones' should be treated as a high priority, not, as is so often the case, a marginal matter which can be postponed indefinitely. Dirt, confusion, decay, disorder, and poisoned atmosphere are the things which have driven many families away from the cities. Many people, who, like myself, have the kind of job which enables them to live in and beyond the green belt, have retreated there to save their children's health and to safeguard their future. Not only is the new housing in the city, as opposed to the suburbs, largely working-class in character, but more importantly the public institutions which serve such areas are invariably sub-standard and inefficient. The schools are often housed in outmoded victorian barracks. There discouraged teachers battle against the apathy of parents and the illiteracy of homes where, as one minister of religion put it, 'books are so seldom in view that in twenty years' visiting you remember the occasions and houses where you saw any'.

At the moment it is generally assumed that inner residential districts will be occupied by lower status groups. But this is a viewpoint I would like to challenge. Middle-class families and those who seek consciously for a better way of life will, it is assumed, either commute to new neighbourhoods or seek salvation in the suburbs. Planners will, of course, try to do all they can to meet the physical and social needs of these older areas, *but there seems to be no intention of trying to develop them as cross-sections of the British community*.

Thus, the pattern of the future will be set in the mould of existing class and income differences. Snobbery, mis-understanding, mutual incomprehension, discrimination, and hostility will be the results of such a policy.

In Liverpool, Manchester, Glasgow, Newcastle, and elsewhere much demolition and rebuilding remains to be done; but once done, the mould will be set for a century. Before it is too late, could we not experiment here and there with the enthusiasm, imagination, and energy which has been devoted to the creation of our post-war New Towns? Let us try, as a beginning, to create in one or two of our great cities the physical and cultural conditions which will attract business and professional people, artists and students, artisans and operatives, to live side by side and share in such aspects of the communal life as are meaning-ful to them. The concert hall, the theatre, the cinema belong to everyone. It is entirely wrong that we should go on running single-class schools in the heart of single-class neighbourhoods. It is surely unchristian moreover for christians to worship only or predominantly with people in the same or similar social strata. At least we should try to avoid such segregation by our planning policies, not to encourage it. Planners and civic architects are, or should be, the servants not the masters of the community. We should tell them that social justice demands not only equality of opportunity for self-advancement, but also equality of environment and the possibility of meeting and sharing experiences with fellow citizens of all kinds. We are, after all, concerned to create the 'good society', not the happy class hide-out. Differentials of income and style there may well be, but these differences can be made to enrich social life not to poison it. I see little hope for democracy, until planning becomes truly democratic. Or, to put it another way, there is little hope of achieving a soundly balanced and truly free and equal community until we plan to live corporate rather than separate lives. Ideals of social justice demand that we should not build our future homes and neighbourhoods on the basis of division and differences. If we do not want to emphasise class and cultural distinctions we must at least see to it that purely physical barriers don't continue to separate us against our will and keep us apart by force. If we wish to love our neighbour, moats won't help!

5
Family and social life in transition

The redevelopment of our towns and cities goes on apace. It is no local affair and has the most far-reaching implications for the future structure of British society. To destroy the old and build the new environment is to do much more than establish a more healthy and adequate human habitat; it is, in a large measure, to determine the quality and extent of social contacts and relationships for generations to come. Since the end of the last war we have put up something like four and a quarter million new homes in this country.* New towns have sprung up to accommodate what we sometimes inelegantly call urban 'overspill' population, and new housing estates have been tacked on to existing centres to cope with expanding numbers and meet the demands of people to possess a home of their own. What has been taking place, and is, indeed, still going on is nothing less than a gigantic nation-wide social experiment, involving whole neighbourhoods and vast populations on the move and under the constraint of enforced change. It is a matter of profound disappointment, to say the least, that civic and national leaders have under-

* i.e., by 1963

taken this huge enterprise without, at the same time, having the whole process studied and documented while it actually was taking place. Not only could on-the-spot sociological research workers have made a contribution to ideas about physical plans and layouts, they could surely have helped the architects and engineers to avoid some of the serious mistakes that flowed from their initial false assumptions. Britain being Britain, the onus of promoting research into the various social problems involved in urban renewal and redevelopment operations was left until recently to the voluntary bodies, the big trusts and foundations on the one hand and the university departments of social science and councils of social service on the other. In the past few years, however, there have been signs of a changed view in official quarters and that grounds for hoping that public policy will come to rely more and more upon the findings of empirical investigation before vital decisions are made. The fact that the Ministry of Housing now has its own sociological research section is an indication that a more enlightened attitude is slowly gaining ground.

The question, then, of what happens to people who have lived in the older urban centres and who are moved to new housing projects is of major human interest. The happiness and mental health of hundreds of thousands of people depend upon the way in which these large-scale migrations take place. Some of the older social problems may be ameliorated by giving families better accommodation and improved facilities. At the same time, it has to be acknowledged, too rapid changes bewilder and upset some people and may make their latter state worse than their former.

It is frequently complained, for example, that life on new housing estates is so different from the old order, so isolated and cut off from friends and relatives that housewives in particular develop a condition sometimes referred to as 'suburban neurosis'. We are told that new residents are often standoffish and suspicious of one another, that they vie in the acquisition of 'status symbols' and possessions. Above all there is the complaint of loneliness and lack of social activities. People are said to sit night after night in the semi-darkness of the boxlike sitting-rooms staring at television sets all night long, seldom going out to meet other people or to enjoy social activities. Ministers of religion and other community workers complain, at the same time, that they can hardly drag folk from the fastness of their own hearthside, that they are not interested in the programmes offered at local church halls or centres. The generalised picture of life in the new out-county estates is often extremely depressing and off-putting. It amounts in the main to a kind of suburban hell, a mental, social and spiritual wilderness made up of neat houses, trim gardens, and with open spaces, in sharp contradistinction to the dilapidated neighbourhoods of the old city centres, where everybody is friendly and people have a deep feeling of belonging in spite of all physical shortcomings.

While these two stereotypes of the 'suburban desert' and the 'snug friendly slum' are obvious exaggerations, they are sufficiently widely held to be worth examining. Members of the community research section of the Department of Social Science, Liverpool University, undertook a survey in the new housing estate of Kirkby, some eight miles from the city, to see how far this image squared up with the facts.

They had already taken a good look at an area of some 48,000 population located in the old residential heart of the city[1] and had found that there was a general dearth of interest in organised social activities although association with the various churches was surprisingly high. Nevertheless, the surveyed area, to which, it will be remembered, we gave the name Crown Street, was anything but a homogeneous community enjoying a common pattern of social and familial life. It seemed to be much more like an accumulation of very small units or fragments of either potential or disrupted communities. Some families were found with wide kinship networks and a long association with a particular locality; others seemed to be comparatively isolated and migrant in character. To sum up, the older residential district in the heart of Liverpool typified in the Crown Street survey was not one big happy family such as Hilda Jennings found the Barton Hill district of Bristol to be[2]. It was exceedingly mixed, varied and diffuse; although features of the 'associative type of society' were observable in some parts, there were also other sectors where isolation and 'anomie' were in evidence.

One of the main items of interest in the Crown Street district survey was residents' desire to have fresh accommodation and their degree of willingness to remain locally or move farther afield. It was found that while some two-thirds wanted to remain or be rehoused locally, about a third were willing, some even eager, to move elsewhere.

[1] Vereker, Mays, Gittus, and Broady, *Urban Redevelopment and Social Change*, Liverpool University Press (1961). See also pp. 60–71 above.

[2] Jennings, *Societies in the Making*, London, Routledge and Kegan Paul (1962).

It seemed, therefore, worth while following up a group of ex-Crown Street residents into their new environments to find out how they were faring and what they felt about their new experiences. It was accordingly decided to ascertain how many ex-Crown Streeters had moved to the Kirkby estate so that with their co-operation a comparison could be made between life in these two strikingly different social environments. Above all the research workers were interested to discover if the quality of ex-Crown Streeters' lives had deteriorated in any significant ways and whether the typical image of the new estate suburban desert held true for them.

A sample containing 108 households was eventually drawn from the city Housing Department's records of families that had moved from Crown Street to Kirkby up to the end of 1959. A schedule of questions was prepared based on the original Crown Street enquiry but slanted towards property and more concerned with attitudes towards neighbours and other social factors than the original questionnaire had been. The results of this enquiry have recently been analysed, and, although by no means complete, sufficient information is available to discuss certain relevant aspects of the great experiment which these 108 households took part in when they left the teeming life of the overcrowded Liverpool streets behind them and embraced a new way of life in the carefully planned but raw neighbourhoods of windswept Kirkby.

At this point it is necessary to point out that so far as this article is concerned all comments regarding attitudes and experiences of the new arrivals are confined to the sample of ex-Crown Streeters studied. Their views and histories cannot be made the basis of generalisations about the population of Kirkby as a whole. They may prove to be untypical in any number of ways and it would hence be dangerous to assume that their reactions are likely to be identical or congruent with those of other new housing estate dwellers in south-west Lancashire or in other parts of the country.

What we can say of them, however, is that their experiences are probably typical of most of the families who used to live in central Liverpool but have recently migrated to Kirkby. Within this limited universe, the findings are of both practical and theoretical value. In so far as this transition has been accomplished without severe strain or breakdown on the part of the majority of the migrants we can say that it has been socially successful. We can then go on to argue that the new housing estate as such is not doomed to failure. If this can be shown on the basis of the evidence available, important lessons may be learned for social policy and administration which may ultimately prove to be valid in other areas and in different conurbations.

It is now time to consider the research findings for the new Kirkby families in greater detail and to contrast them wherever possible with the life of the older city neighbourhoods from which they came.

In the first place it was found, as might have been expected, that the ex-Crown Street households now living in Kirkby contained a much higher proportion of young children than had been the case in the old inner city wards. Heads of households were also on average much younger. This again was expected on the basis of the fact that in the earlier survey it had been the younger families which had been the most ready to move. Not only were the new families younger in composition and hence possibly more vigorous than their Crown Street counterparts had been on average in the earlier survey, but they were also apparently more sociable. Members of families were associated with a considerable number of social groups and organisations ranging from those attached to churches and political parties to clubs specifically for women or old age pensioners. Significantly, more new Kirkby households (44%) claimed to have at least one member attached to such groups than when they had resided in central Liverpool. This was a surprising discovery which goes a considerable way towards modifying the stereotype of the lonely dormitory suburb. Moreover, while cinema attendance had slumped, participation in activities associated with churches and attendance at religious services had not. In the original Crown Street survey 45% of the households were said to be in touch with some worshipping community or another. In the new Kirkby households the figure stood at no less than 43% for attendance at church services alone. There had obviously been no dramatic decline in church attendance following on the migration as might have been expected in view of the statements frequently made by parsons in new housing estates, who have sometimes reported a complete, though temporary, breakdown of external religious associations amongst new arrivals.

Undoubtedly, one of the reasons why the religious association and practice of the ex-Crown Streeters were so satisfactorily maintained was that the churches themselves were, in the main, ready for the invasion and had got the nucleus of their organisation in being before all the new population arrived. In particular, the Roman Catholic churches evidenced considerable foresight and vitality.

Not only has the Roman Catholic Church concentrated on building the necessary schools and chapels to meet the residents' needs, it has gone much further by establishing the necessary halls and clubs so that the parish could become as much a focus for the social life of the neighbourhoods as for the more narrowly religious activities. Immense energy has been devoted to this achievement and funds have been raised on an impressive scale. In fairness it must be stated that the Church of England has also, though at a somewhat slower pace, striven to meet the needs of its people at all levels. In 1963–4, for example, they put up an entirely new Youth Centre for the use of young people of all denominations or none.

Had the Catholic Church not been ready for the waves of new arrivals who descended upon Kirkby from its inception in 1952 to its virtual completion in the early 1960's, social life might have well have broken down entirely. No less than half the entire population is catholic. This fact, together with the unprecedented rate of occupation (Kirkby passed from being a tiny rural village to the proportions of an entire New Town in less than a decade!) presented the most widespread and urgent problems. Added to the many problems arising out of strangeness and mere newness have been the high rates of unemployment and, in the early years, the absence of shops and similar basic amenities. Kirkby was not only a housing estate cast in the mould of a statutory New Town, but lacking the status and support that the latter would have entailed, it was also an estate in a desperate hurry. The basis of allocation of houses was solely people's need for accommodation. This resulted in the creation of a one-class area with a vast preponderance of manual workers.

Inevitably amongst such a mass of ex-urban families coming from the poorer and slummier parts of Liverpool there has been a proportion of families exhibiting serious problems. Their numbers have often been exaggerated so that to its many other difficulties the young urban district council (set up in 1957) has something of a social stigma to overcome.

But as will be apparent from the foregoing, Kirkby has offered the ex-Crown Streeters a viable environment and the prospect of a life of fairly adequate standards. True, rather more than half the households interviewed already expressed dissatisfaction with their new accommodation. Fifty-eight per cent wanted to leave their dwelling but only 34 % wanted to get out of Kirkby altogether. In the main this dissatisfied minority disliked the accommodation and the locality rather than their neighbours. Only 6% gave dissatisfaction with neighbours as a reason for wanting to leave. The long journey to work, the unfamiliarity of landmarks, the dislike of flats, the feeling of being cut off from the main stream of life—these were almost certainly factors producing a general sense of unrest and dissatisfaction. It is almost certain that any estate in any part of the country would reveal a similar unsettled minority.

For the majority of ex-inner city dwellers the new estate is desirable or at least adequate. Certainly the residents as a whole did not seem to be unusually isolated. Fifty-four per cent of the households claimed to go out with members of other households in their locality. This was in addition to the informal, unplanned, casual contact between residents in the streets, shops, and clinics which must inevitably have multiplied the degree of social interaction

4*

considerably. Only 29% found their neighbours less friendly in Kirkby than they had found their neighbours in Crown Street. Eighty-four per cent said they 'got on' with their neighbours, which indicates that even those who found them less friendly than in the old neighbourhood did not find them offensive. Nor were there any signs that the move outside the city had seriously reduced the quality of contact with relatives and kinsfolk. Although 57% of the households agreed that they nowadays saw less of their relatives, and only 12% saw more of them, they still seemed to keep in touch. In particular, illness or some other crisis appeared to bring them into close association once again, although contact of the 'popping in and out' kind had naturally ended. As a generalisation it would be true to say that the kinship relationship was tending to become even more of a latent or quiescent force, activated by sudden emergencies, but in the main not expressed in close contact. This increasing importance of the two-generation household in the main living its own life and coping with its own problems, sometimes with the help of kin and sometimes with the help of a statutory and voluntary service, is very much in line with the general pattern for family living in Britain in the second part of the twentieth century. It coincides with other tendencies which have sometimes been described as a general approximation of the traditional middle-class way of life.

This study of a selected group of residents living in Kirkby is necessarily superficial. The method of study involving statistical sampling of households by routine questionnaire method is not likely to produce the more subtle 'depth' material which would be necessary to paint a complete picture of what it means to leave the older neighbourhoods and start putting down roots in a distant suburb. But sketchy as it is, it does help us to revise some of the more exaggerated ideas associated with new estates. Kirkby has suffered acute disadvantages: it has equally enjoyed unusual benefits. Had it been a New Town designated it would have a more balanced community and perhaps greater access to employment. At the same time it had from the very beginning its own considerable trading estate, the relic of a wartime factory which the city of Liverpool has sought to develop by every possible means. It is significant that while only 2% of our sample households had jobs in the new housing estate when they originally moved, by the time the interviewing took place (1960), this figure had risen to 21%. This may well increase and we are entitled to suppose that it will form an increasingly important stabilising factor in the life of the young township. Opinion is beginning to swing back from the idea that work and residence should be widely separated to the idea that they should lie more or less conveniently contiguous, and, in this respect, Kirkby certainly scores over the ordinary housing estate, which often has little or no indigenous employment to offer its residents.

Social and family life at any rate is revealed as being far from denuded by the changeover. Group activities continue and expand. The churches clearly play a dominant role in the developing community life of the neighbourhoods. Moreover, the more recent completion of the civic and shopping centre should help to nourish a sense of communal pride and, as the years go by, such institutions and amenities should serve to deflect the backward looking gaze of ex-Liverpudlians towards the growing prospect of a healthy and distinctive corporate existence. The break up of old ties and associations is for these ex-Crown Streeters seen as a less traumatic experience than a similar uprooting was for the residents of the Barton Hill area of Bristol, who undoubtedly experienced considerable pain in making the compulsory transition from an old community of Barton Hill, with families deeply rooted and anchored to a few parochial areas, with firm links over the generations reinforced by the interlocking of many kinship networks and a strongly developed sense of local community spirit. Our sample of households derived from a much less ordered and culturally uniform urban background. To this extent they were freer to make the change and face the hazards of a strange and new way of living. It is clear furthermore that two other factors have helped and are likely to help even more so in the future to weld Kirkby together into a stable community. These are respectively the extent of church activities and loyalties on the one hand and on the other the fact that Kirkby has shaken free of the Liverpool's apron strings. Kirkby has not only attained local authority status a few years after its inception, but it now has its own council of social service to act as a focal point for voluntary endeavour. For all its undoubted problems it is a place of hope and confidence. We cannot but feel that, in the end, the long trek from the dingy cramped backstreets of central Liverpool to the bracing expanse of 'Newtown' will prove for its recent arrivals a step towards higher status and a happier and fuller life.

6
Social disadvantage and education

In the last three chapters we discussed various social deprivations and family disadvantages arising from the fact that comparatively large sections of the population are still obliged (even in a so-called affluent society) to live in inadequate physical conditions, and we outlined some of the serious problems associated with this fact. Now we will consider in more detail, in this and the following chapter, what the educational consequences are for children who have to grow up in a substandard environment. In recent years two significant government reports (*Half Our Future*, 1963, and *Children and Their Primary Schools*, 1967, both prepared by the Central Advisory Council for Education (England), and now usually referred to more simply after the names of their chairmen as *Newsom* and *Plowden*) have highlighted some of the grosser problems facing schools in socially underprivileged areas. These two reports have been widely debated in professional educational circles and warmly received, but so far very little government action has yet been taken to implement their recommendations. This is a deplorable fact, and one which any responsible citizen should become aware of, for the simple reason that today the kind of education an individual receives almost entirely determines his future prospects and social destiny. Education is at once the great social liberator and the great social divider. Hence those who are concerned about the quality of public life in contemporary Britain must come to terms with the moral and social implications of our present educational system. Above all, the problem facing schools in disadvantaged neighbourhoods should receive our most detailed scrutiny, for it may very well be that many of the social problems— such as poverty, lack of skill, unemployment, juvenile delinquency, and certain kinds of mental ill-health (to name just a few of the things which afflict even our technologically sophisticated society)—have their origins in early educational failure and consequent occupational and financial frustration which the socially handicapped experience at the very outset of their lives.

The 1944 Education Act has rightly been called a revolutionary document, establishing as it did in so forthright a manner the unprecedented principle of secondary education for all, irrespective of class, ability, or financial means. Since it was placed on the statute book argument has raged over how it should be implemented. More recently political parties have competed for public approval for their somewhat divergent views as to how true educational equality is to be achieved. Meanwhile the professional educationalists have argued about the accuracy of selective techniques. They have lamented the high proportion of early leavers. But, in the heat of the discussion the rights and needs of the less able and less fortunate children have often been misunderstood. Administrators have tended to think of their plight as in the main one of inadequate facilities and scant resources—weaknesses that time, money, and planning could ultimately remove. Teachers, perhaps, have been misled into believing that better techniques of instruction and smaller and more homogeneous classes would reduce the proportions of the problem until we would eventually be left with the residue of the intellectually less gifted pupils for whom some kind of special school instruction would be most equitable. Most are well aware that, at the moment, the idea of equal opportunity is a hollow mockery. If it means anything, it means simply that children from vastly unequal backgrounds have an equal chance to compete for what rewards and resources are available. But the time will come, so it is hoped, when these inequalities will be eliminated and we will enjoy an educational system based on both justice and equality.

There is a minority, however, who would question the logic of so amiable an argument. As practitioners they know that not only is parity a polite fiction but also that equality of opportunity cannot be achieved even at some distant date while it continues to be associated with innate mental endowment. Experience over many years has demonstrated the paramount importance of the family in developing a child's innate talents. Not only the home but also the locality in which it is situated exerts a profound effect on how a child, and his parents, view schooling and what their general attitude towards higher and further education is likely to be. We know moreover that some schools have more capable staffs than others, that some primary departments have a proud record of achievement in the 11 + examination while others have a tradition of failure. This being the case, true equality of opportunity demands that handicaps with which pupils start on their educational career should be redressed. To do this, the schools with the poorer records and traditions will have to be brought up to the level of those which have a high morale derived from academic success.

To some extent this is a viable administrative possibility. Careful selection of teachers for the less satisfactory schools, and inducements to them to go there, and the re-furbishing and re-equipment of buildings and classrooms to bring them into line with modern requirements, would together go some way towards reducing the gap between the academically more and less successful primary departments. Formidable differences and disadvantages would however still remain that no amount of redeployment of purely educational resources would obviate. Schools do not operate in a social vacuum. They are always part and parcel of their neighbourhoods and are profoundly influenced by the ideas and attitudes institutionalised in the surrounding milieux. They are also to a great extent functionally related to the wider social structure. Behind every local council or church school lies an unseen continent of national history which has made them what they are and which cannot be obliterated by the stroke of the pen or even by act of parliament.

The question that the educational sociologist is currently deeply interested in is how these purely social influences operate and condition what goes on in every classroom, and, more particularly, why in some localities the influence of formal education is so slight by comparison with other areas. Not enough is known in an objective way about the social forces operating within the local milieu and, until we know what these are and how they come into being, little effective action can be taken to neutralise any adverse influences.

It should be emphasised that I am talking here about a minority, but an important and a substantial one. That there are thousands of educationally disadvantaged children in this country today, in spite of the 1944 Act, cannot be denied. The teachers and administrators know where they exist. In the many cases they are to be found living in the old, central, residential zones of the major cities and conurbations, in what in the old days used to be called 'the slums'. The proportion of children in the appropriate age groups from such districts who gain selective secondary school places is staggeringly lower than for similar schools in the suburbs. The difference in broad terms may be stated as between 5% and 10% in the inner districts contrasted with 50% to 70% in the better-off wards. Here resistance to the efforts of the schools is in the shape of inertia rather than open hostility. As we said in Chapter 3, it is a negative attitude towards the schools rather than a positive repudiation of what they stand for. The standards that the schools in these older down-town urban neighbourhoods are striving to uphold are often alien to those exemplified in the local community. I want to illustrate this by quoting from a study made of the work of some secondary modern and primary schools in a central residential area of Liverpool[1]. While this may be somewhat different, at least in detail, from under-privileged neighbourhoods in other parts of the country, I believe that it is sufficiently representative of the major

[1] J. B. Mays, *Education and the Urban Child*, Liverpool University Press (1962).

characteristics which deeply influence the work of the schools.

The following comments are extracted from a chapter discussing the nature of the local subculture. The immediate point of departure is the field worker's reaction to a Display and At Home. 'Such displays seem alien to the locality and, out of the context of the school, completely unreal. How many of these girls who don school uniforms during the day go out at night in tight-fitting skirts to jive and rock? What do they think then of country dancing and songs about cuckoos and linden leas?'

One cannot help feeling that much of the culture being offered in such schools is archaic and can have little or no significance in the minds of these children in the busy, dirty streets and in the high tenement blocks which stand on the edges of rubble-strewn wastelands in the centre of the run-down city. Teachers are urged to make use of the local environment to give point to their lessons. What can they do in such circumstances? How can they evoke interest in children who are bored by the gasworks and the railway coalyard and not a bit interested in nightingales either? In an area characterised by racial confusion and hostility, high delinquency and illegitimacy rates, where the air is blackened with fumes and grit and smoke, where the days are noisy and dangerous and the nights conceal more stealthy vices, where do archetypal figures like Peter Pan and Hiawatha fit? Admittedly this is an extreme picture, but the fact is that, as a society, we are still living in the long twilight of the Two Nations, but the divided classes are no longer the rich and the poor, the obviously privileged and nakedly underprivileged of former times. Between teacher and child is a wide cultural gulf. It is the same gulf which used to divide the elementary from the grammar school tradition. Old customs and habits die hard. Suspicions of discrimination and possible unemployment are still active in many minds, while the children have not inherited a stable pattern of behaviour. The shadow of the long years of former scarcity still lies across the old slums like a defensive veil which teachers find difficult to penetrate. Not many people look towards the schools for the foundation of their future careers. Few see the social and financial advantages that education can confer. They submit to, but do not gladly embrace, compulsory education up to fifteen. Not many seek further training after schooldays are over. Only a small minority of parents take an active interest in examinations or show concern about their children's academic progress. When schooldays are over there are enough jobs offering good wages at the moment. The girls can go to the local clothing factory or the football pool firms. For the boys there is unskilled manual labour, or a seafaring job is usually to be had.

In such working-class districts life is focussed on two vital points—the home and the neighbourhood. Horizons are narrow, ambitions severely limited to the local and the concrete. Home is still a fairly tightly-knit group of relatives surrounded by an outer fringe of neighbours who, however, seldom cross the threshold. Neighbours borrow from one another. Standoffishness is not liked, nor is parsimony respected. Life is social in the narrow sense that people dislike doing things on their own. 'They go through life with their arms linked, holding one another up', said a local headteacher critically. On the other hand the security and comfort afforded by group life cannot lightly be dismissed as valueless. Young people are especially gregarious and are invariably to be seen in groups and small clusters. They so dislike being cut off from their friends that many do not want to do well in the General Entrance Examination and they make no effort.

The work of the social services is taken for granted and avidly exploited in such areas. Hard-pressed parents leave as much as they can to the teacher, the youth employment officer, the club leader, the nurse, and the play centre supervisor. Not many parents bother to attend school-leavers' conferences, very few ask for homework, and the link between teacher and parent is very tenuous. Positive resistance is confined to a handful who neglect their children and absenteeism tends to run in families. But many of the 'good' parents spoil their offspring. The early years of childhood lack discipline and essential routine. As one experienced teacher put it, 'Children rule round here. The mothers bribe them, the fathers are not interested, and the kids do very much what they like.'

One of the reasons for this state of affairs is the fact that the family is victorian in character and male and female roles are sharply differentiated. Housework and child care are traditionally feminine responsibilities, while the man's duty is to bring home the money, deal out exemplary punishment when necessary, and in his off-duty hours enjoy himself relaxing either at the local pub or at the football match. The girls are expected to do a lot of work in the home and to take a share in looking after the younger ones. Boys are by contrast much more free. They may run errands or do paper rounds, but like their dads they expect to have ample leisure and amusement. Even the meals are eaten individually rather than *en famille*. Family life therefore tends to be segmented, not lacking in warmth or intimacy, but by its structure unsuited to exert uniform discipline, or to promote common decision-making or corporate action. The mothers seem particularly burdened, with little relief from toil and few social outlets. Families tend to be larger here than the national average, and the cramped, often totally inadequate, flats and houses make housekeeping a drudgery. It has, moreover, often to be carried out over and above doing a part-time job. In cases where husbands are away from home or have deserted, the burden can often become excessive and without the help of the social services it is difficult to see how some of the mothers could manage at all.

In general, therefore, we may say that the pattern of life in the localities which do badly academically, and from which few children gain selective secondary school places, is the antithesis of the carefully organised middle-class existence, and, in so far as this is true, is not geared up to secondary education as it has developed in the past hundred years in this country. The reasons behind the poor examination performance of so many average and above-average pupils are therefore highly complicated and not amenable to quick administrative remedies. The typical mental attitudes which have emerged over long years of close community association in a condition of comparative poverty are narrowly hedonistic, unambitious and group-centred. They will not change quickly or easily. Alterations of the social structure, increased opportunities, the provision of modern buildings and new institutional arrangements will not by themselves be strong enough to dissolve the hard core of a deeply entrenched social conservatism which burdens these old slum neighbourhoods. The problem that they present is exceptionally challenging, therefore, and should evoke a comparably whole-hearted remedial response from the entire educational profession. Simple human justice demands that this state of affairs should not be left as it is: otherwise, as other social groups advance, the latter state of the people who are unlucky enough to be born in these underprivileged areas will be much worse than their former.

The problem that confronts the teacher in the typical down-town school in an underprivileged community is thus psycho-social in nature. It is one with which, in the main, he is not trained to deal nor is it indeed a purely school or educational problem. So wide and complex are the many factors which interweave to create the 'problem school in the problem area' that the teacher may well feel they are altogether beyond his competence. Some teachers, who become aware of the almost impermeable barrier of hostility and indifference with which they have to contend, resolve their difficulties by seeking transfers to the more responsive schools in the suburban neighbourhoods. There is a flight not only of pupils but also of teachers from many slum schools, as the authors of the Crowther Report clearly indicated. Thus the typical pattern of inequality is built up and maintained. Give a school a bad reputation and it will increasingly seem to deserve its stigma. Only concerted and carefully thought out administrative and individual action can reverse the process and redress the adverse balance in such deprived localities. Considerations of simple human justice and decency, however, demand that a strenuous effort should be made to eliminate the grosser causes of educational wastage and failure.

There are two principal spheres within which direct

action might usefully commence: the first lies within the local school and neighbourhood and involves a reshaping of the teacher's traditional role. The second is the province of the educational authorities as such and is fundamentally a matter of more adequate physical provision and a redeployment of the financial and human resources within their control.

Within the down-town school itself it is necessary that the teaching staff should accept an extension of their role and undertake as part of their task the promotion of what sociologists call 'social change'. That is to say they should become active participants in the equalisation and democratisation process and express their commitment to those values, social and moral, which underpin the 1944 Act. By accepting a programme of social welfare as their overall objective they may in fact be rewarded by finding that their purely educational and scholastic functions will be all the more effective as a result of enlisting a greater measure of support and understanding from the surrounding community.

All this means that teachers will have to concern themselves not just with the children in their classrooms but with the whole life of the neighbourhood. For the attitudes and standards of the children do not exist in isolation and hence cannot be dealt with out of context. The atmosphere of each individual home and the general culture of the district must be taken into account in everything they do. Those influences which at the moment are clearly seen to be inimical to educational purposes and intransigent to most pedagogic efforts will have to be identified and transformed into the potentially powerful allies that they undoubtedly are.

Schools should strive to make themselves the focal point of local community effort, welfare and education. The beginnings of such a service are already in being in the close association that exists between teachers, youth employment officials, and school medical officers and nurses. What is now required is an extension of this kind of work to embrace more and more of the neighbourhood's life. The centring of evening classes, play centres, and youth organisations on the school building are obvious first steps that could be taken to achieve this end. The task is, of course, a tremendous one and calls for devoted and determined service on the part of the teachers. But the logic of reality in these underprivileged areas demands that it be attempted. As so many teachers know, school is the only sheet anchor in these neighbourhoods for a great number of children and families, the one reliable source of guidance, encouragement, and support. All this means something much more thoroughgoing than the orthodox parent-teacher association with its whist drives and socials. It means reaching out to the adults of the district in an endeavour to assist them to cope more adequately with such problems as absenteeism, truancy, backwardness, discipline of children, supervision of leisure, preparation for parenthood, job selection, and vocational training—a gigantic and inclusive programme which far outsoars the conventional job of formal class instruction in a list of subjects on a prescribed syllabus! Much experimentation in the field of parent-teacher co-operation will have to take place and no ideal pattern is likely to be discovered which can be imposed mechanically in every locality. One thing is quite clear and that is that the teachers can no longer stay immured in their classrooms but must go out into the streets and the homes and make a positive approach to parents to get them to understand the issues involved and to elicit their support. It may even be necessary in some schools to appoint special teacher-social workers whose task it would be to encourage, advise, and, at critical moments, to summon aid for individual families. Whatever methods are chosen they will need to be flexible and informal and yet, at the same time, sufficiently stable and enduring to build up confidence over the years and offer a reliable bulwark against social disintegration.

Clearly teachers cannot be expected to do all this additional work and shoulder all this extra responsibility without a considerable amount of support both locally and nationally. One major contribution that the authorities can make is to explode what we might call the 'myth of the blackboard jungle', to demolish the fairly widely held view that teaching in these down-town schools is a nightmare of hostility and indiscipline. Those who have experience of working in such schools know that it is far from being the case that the suburbs have all the advantages on their side. The alleged lack of response is often greatly exaggerated; while the notion that the status of the teacher is held in derision is absurdly untrue. It is a matter of great educational importance not only that wrong ideas of what is involved in working in these older schools should be dispelled but that, further, the local education authority should give them urgent priority for staffing and equipment. Moreover, the government must act quickly and generously in providing the necessary funds to demolish the existing inadequate premises and replace them with up-to-date buildings which will be attractive to pupils and teachers alike, and so help to boost the morale of the entire neighbourhood by visibly demonstrating that we are really in earnest about the value of education.

The staffing problem can be helped if authorities would stress the importance of work in the poorer secondary modern and primary schools. While financial inducements alone, as suggested by the Crowther Committee, might be undesirable, an alternative suggestion, that promotion should entail a satisfactory spell of work in the difficult neighbourhood, has much to recommend it. Whatever can be done, however, to arouse the missionary zeal of the teaching profession should be attempted, for there are still reserves of devotion and vocational enthusiasm waiting to be tapped and directed to the needs of these less fortunate areas. Special attention to the problems of such districts could very well be given in training to help young teachers to make the necessary mental adjustments required by such arduous work. The growth of sociology teaching in training colleges is greatly to be welcomed, provided it is in the right hands and is not tied down to a somewhat narrow academicism. Lectures and tutorials devoted to the findings of social surveys of contemporary living conditions are greatly to be preferred to erudite enquiry, for example, into what Weber meant by 'life style'. But the findings of empirical enquiries into significant social problems and descriptions of differing patterns of family life and associated attitudes would be invaluable in interpreting the significance of subcultural distinctions to young teachers and, with good tutorial assistance, should enable them to make their techniques more flexible and their methods more easily adaptable to changing circumstances.

The various possible steps that might be taken to give

the down-town schools new vitality might usefully be summarised under the following heads:

(a) the provision of new and better equipped buildings;
(b) the recruitment of academically better qualified teaching staff;
(c) the development of a strong functional link between school and home, employing positive techniques for eliciting parental support;
(d) the elimination of wastage of talent and ability;
(e) the provision of adequate recreational facilities in close association with the school centre;
(f) instruction for teachers during training in social background data derived from sociological research.

In isolation none of these recommendations will take us very far. But in combination, as part of a concerted national programme, they could make a useful beginning to the herculean task of making our educational system more equal and democratic. New buildings themselves will prove ineffective; adequate equipment and extended facilities can easily fail because of human and psychological deficiencies. To be successful, change must operate more or less simultaneously on two distinct but closely related levels. We must change the physical setting in which education occurs, and, equally vital, we must change people's attitudes and ideas about what is going on in the schools. And when we say change people's attitudes, we must not confine this to the children and their parents. Teachers themselves need renewed hope and the impetus of fresh vision. They must forget their prejudices and ruthlessly discard outmoded notions of slum children's so-called 'basic inferiority'.

But behind the whole process sleeps the inertia of public opinion. Neither government nor the community of citizens as a whole are deeply or whole-heartedly enough committed to education to produce the revolution implicit and, indeed, explicitly mentioned in the 1944 Act. Until they are, teachers and educational administrators must soldier along determinedly. Perhaps their most useful contribution will ultimately be found to lie in the publicity they themselves agree to give to their own problems and the energy with which, both in and out of season, they stress the vital human, social and economic issues which are bound up with their work.

Part 3

Crime and punishment

7
Crime and society

Perhaps the first thing we ought to say about crime in general is that it is apparently on the increase, and all the indications are that it will continue to increase in the future unless really drastic changes occur in the structure and character of our society. Criminal statistics are notoriously haphazard and unreliable for most comparative purposes, but, even allowing for all the known sources of discrepancy arising from different methods of recording, for changes in the climate of public opinion and actual alterations in the law itself, it is clear that, compared with a little more than a quarter of a century ago, we are something like twice as criminal in our behaviour. The population has increased by not more than 12% during that time, while the total number of offences known to the police has gone up by over a hundred per cent. We now top the million mark for indictable offences, and the annual total still seems to be rising, although the proportionate increase has tended to fall somewhat in the past year or so. Non-indictable offences also show a steady rise, but to a lesser degree than the indictable, which are of course generally regarded as the more serious kinds of offences. But, among the latter, it may be noted that 'taking and driving away' cars is included, and since this type of offence can have extremely grave side-effects, some criminologists are of the opinion that it ought now to become indictable and be much more severely dealt with than it has been in the past.

Altogether the outlook is unpropitious. With an annual increase in crime of between 6% and 10% it is difficult to be complacent about the future or unconcerned by current trends. Crimes against property using violence are going up, as is violence against the person. Robbery is on the increase, and so is the net cash value of every robbery. It has been estimated that in London alone a sum of no less than £2 million a year is stolen by organised criminals. One of the most widely discussed features in recent years is the apparent growth of criminality amongst the young. The peak age for indictable crimes remains around the fourteenth birthday, although, more recently, as far as non-indictable, non-motoring offences go, the older teenagers between seventeen and twenty bulk largest. Railway offences, usually involving dishonesty, malicious damage, and assaults, probably account for this new peak. But, more seriously, in the indictable area, the fifteen-year-olds seem to be equalling the thirteen-year-olds, and a secondary peak is appearing in later adolescence round about the seventeenth birthday. Criminal behaviour seems not only to be the special prerogative of male children but is also becoming the province of young men up to the age of twenty-one or so—that is to say, it is increasingly being associated with the period of biological and social im-maturity, and this fact, I think, gives us an important clue to the nature of the complex relationship between crime and society. To a very considerable extent it seems that criminal behaviour of various kinds is associated with irresponsibility and unregulated personal freedom, or, as some would prefer to say, with a decrease of discipline and an increase of leisure time amongst children and young people, and with our own increasing sensitivities.

Although there is obviously a great deal of adult crime and juvenile delinquency in contemporary society, it would be wrong to talk about this, as some people do, as a crime wave. It is much more like a chronic condition closely associated with some of the typical institutions and ingrained ideas of our entire culture pattern. The plain truth of the matter is that most crime and practically all delinquency is committed by ordinary people, not by lunatics or outlaws. The total bulk of offences may be divided between the amateurs and the professionals. The latter are few in number, but their premeditated villainies account for the most daring and larger robberies, of which the famous mail train robbery will remain for very many years as the frightening prototype. But the growth of protection rackets, associated with the legalisation of gaming, especially in the London area, suggests how Britain could follow the United States in the direction of large scale criminal organisation unless we are very careful. The smuggling and peddling of narcotics is another, though by no means new, type of professional criminality which attracts the expert crooks and involves a whole number of lesser offenders in its nefarious networks. But the fact remains that most offences are perpetrated by ordinary people, and a majority of those who feature in the official statistics are occasional, minor, and petty offenders, most of whom, for the greater part of their time, are law-abiding and even decent folk. Their crimes and delinquencies are probably more often impulsive than premeditated: they succumb to temptation rather than pursue a life of outlawry; they are more weak than wicked, in some sense the victims of adverse circumstances rather than self-willed enemies of society.

One needs, hence, to differentiate first between professional thieves and villains, who probably comprise less than 5% of all known offenders, and all the others who merely lapse into crime for shorter or longer periods. We must also distinguish between adult and juvenile offenders. The latter are often a tremendous nuisance, but they are seldom a serious menace to the stability and welfare of the community. A great many young offenders are simply lacking in care and discipline; others are in such a state of anxiety or neglect that we can think of their delinquencies as distress signals sent up to summon help or to express their feelings of outrage against a rejecting environment. We need to take their offences very seriously—not to treat them always at their face value, but to probe beneath the presenting symptoms to uncover the personal problems which underlie their rebellious behaviour. This means further subdividing the young offenders into two main groups: one, which comprises the great majority, made up of ordinary youngsters who are kicking over the traces because they are insufficiently cared for; and two, the minority who are so seriously disturbed in the psychological sense, either as a result of parental neglect or some mishap which has upset their family life, or the handful who are genuinely mentally sick in a clinical sense. I don't want to suggest that any of these categories are incapable of taking responsibility for their actions, but I would suggest that each represents a different kind of need which requires a different kind of help and treatment.

There is no time here to launch into an elaborate hypothetical typology of offenders. But I hope I have said enough to show that crime is a very complex phenomenon, not a simple human condition to be equated either with wickedness or immorality. There are many different types of crimes and a whole array of offenders, and for this reason we can seldom talk profitably about crime or delinquency in abstract or general terms. We need to think rather of types of offenders, each of which selects the kind of offence that meets its more basic needs. The big-time crook, like any other big business man, is looking for profits: the sexually inadequate male may seek through exhibitionism his only available biological outlet; the back-street vandal may be looking for adventure; the teenage lout may be searching for kicks; the schoolboy shoplifter may be looking for affection—and so on.

My argument has now led me to a point where I can state that we must try to think of crime and delinquency in much more sophisticated terms than we have done in the past. It is not simply wrongdoing which is to be corrected by punishment. If it were, mankind would have eliminated it long ago. The motivations of offenders are multiple. Hence we must uncover their variety and treat them differently. This is a skilled task which requires all the scientific research and all the sociological and psychological understanding of which we are capable. There are few easy answers and no pat solutions. If we react by getting hot under our moral collars, we will very likely make things worse.

Here I would like to draw attention to a point which the

police have often complained about, the fact that we are not all equally or all the time behind the law and united in our attitude towards criminals and towards crimes. Most of us at one time or another find ourselves up against the authorities, whom we rightly or wrongly perceive as unjust, immoral, and misguided. We are sometimes very hostile to the edicts of the very party we have voted into power. We resent the local authority bye-laws which prevent us putting up that extra garage or adding that bay-window on to our house. The income tax officials are seen as veritable extortionists rather than as public servants, obedient to the majority rule. Motorists caught speeding loathe the police patrol and immediately assume a 'them' against 'us' stance We say that radar traps are unfair. Traffic wardens are snoopers. More seriously, citizens stand aside while a felony is being committed; a bus queue watches a snatch and grab taking place on the other side of the road without taking any action; a policeman is in difficulty controlling a crowd outside a football ground and is treated to jeers and catcalls by the onlookers. I have already mentioned that frightening instance in a New York avenue, when the neighbours looked on while a girl was murdered outside her own front door, when several witnessed the incident and not only failed to ring up for help but simply didn't want to know what was happening. Such instances, grave or trivial, are indicators of cross-currents in the body politic. They contribute in their own underground way to the vast complex of crime in modern society, fostering that secret deviance, as it has been termed, which indirectly supports the network of crime and immorality.

I have just used the terms *crime* and *immorality* together, but of course they ought not to be confused. Immoral acts are not always criminal, nor are all offences necessarily transgressions of the moral code. Whose moral code are we talking about, anyway? The law is comparatively clear where it stands, even if jurists like to argue amongst themselves about detailed interpretations. But when it comes to moral issues we are truly in Tom Tiddler's territory. Some lawyers and some social commentators argue that the function of the law is to regulate social relations, not to control our morals, while others, like Lord Devlin, maintain that the law should underwrite the moral code as the latter may appear to all reasonable men of good will. This is a very thorny topic, but one we cannot ignore in any discussion on the relation between crime and society. The late Sir Norwood East, one of our greatest forensic psychiatrists, who spent a lifetime grappling with the profound psychological and social problems presented by crime, wrote this in his neglected classic, *Society and the Criminal* (London, 1949):

> . . . as the criminologist looks out upon the world, and sees men and women in important positions making false and often unscrupulous assertions in order to secure personal advantage, he can hardly fail to compare their moral turpitude with that of those who break the law.

In my view, we ought to make strenuous efforts to bring morality and the law closer together. It seems to me an undesirable, and in some ways a socially dangerous, condition if these two fundamental aspects of living are often found at variance. The law must change as moral ideas evolve. Thus nowadays, when high placed churchmen no longer condemn homosexual relations as necessarily immoral, we are obliged to bring the law into harmony with this newer attitude. To do otherwise would be to maintain the antagonism and make the law contemptible to some sections of the community. But note, this is not the same as saying that the legal code is to be lightly changed under the influence of fickle swings of public opinion. Neither morality nor law should be the servants of unprincipled opportunism nor subject to mere whims and fads. But there has to be harmony and proportion in our social order so that when, after prolonged deliberation, parliament decides after a majority vote to permit homosexual relations between consenting adults, we have all got to accept this as a reasonable solution to what is, by any assessment, a most tricky moral and social problem. My point is, in a few words, that law ought to support and reinforce morality, but should itself be modifiable as new human understanding and scientific knowledge becomes available to us.

What does worry me quite considerably in our present set-up is not the lifting of legal sanctions against adult homosexuals (of which I am in favour), but rather the fact that a whole series of activities, which seem to me to be highly anti-social and immoral, are not forbidden and punishable by law. There is no space to do more than illustrate what I mean by one or two examples, all, as it happens, drawn from the world of business and finance.

My first example is in the field of business mergers and take-over bids. In some cases these activities are clearly unscrupulous and against the common good. Dr Heenan, when Archbishop of Liverpool, attacked some of these transactions in words which I cannot better: 'It is not unknown', he wrote, 'for firms to be taken over simply to be destroyed. Directors who accept profitable offers without guaranteeing the future welfare of those they employ are plainly immoral.' I would go further and say that all such transactions involving, amongst other inequities, the institution known as the 'golden handshake' should be made illegal. Just as the medieval church condemned the practice of usury as immoral, I believe we ought to bring our civil law up to date by condemning certain kinds of business mergers as being positively detrimental to the common good.

My second example is a practice which has recently been brought more sharply under public scrutiny and control, that is, the institution of expense accounts and associated 'perks'. Many sorts of payment in kind, hidden subsidies, and invisible emoluments need to be strictly controlled, for while the ordinary working man believes that the bosses are secretly lining their own pockets by giving each other slap-up meals at the firm's expense, loaning cars and houses to privileged employees, the general climate of public opinion will remain cynical and opportunist, and will continue to encourage the anti-social idea that 'it's every man for himself', which, in my judgement, is powerfully criminogenic.

Maybe I give the impression of hoping for a utopia in which all men seek to do the right thing for the right reasons and the best of motives. Of course I do, but I am not so foolish as to imagine it is waiting just round the corner. I do, however, think we can bring it one step nearer if we look much more closely at some of our accepted social institutions of which I will be saying more at a later stage in this chapter. But now I want to pass on to another problematic topic, closely related to my main theme, and this concerns the nature of man and poses some sticky philosophical and psychological questions both for the criminologist and the penal reformer. The problem, very simply, is whether or not we are by nature delinquent and anti-social. Some authorities obviously think that we are inherently criminally disposed, and that the whole process of learning is one whereby the stubborn egotist is weaned and prodded into accepting the legal code of his society and the mores of his family group. This is the classical Freudian view. Dr Edward Glover claims that '. . . crime is part of the price paid for the domestication of a naturally wild animal, or, to put it more cautiously, that crime is *one* of the results of unsuccessful domestication'[1]. Other consequences might be the neuroses.

Dr Roper, who was for many years an outstanding member of the staff of Wakefield Prison, puts it rather differently, but he has the same notion that delinquency involves doing more or less what comes naturally:

> The question presents itself: if criminality and immaturity are so closely associated, may they not be much the same thing? We know that young children can be seen, in any not too tidy nursery, assaulting each other, taking the belongings of others, and even engaging in sexual exploration, in a way which would be criminal in adults. No sensible person worries about these things because he knows that it is a normal phase of development which will disappear with training. May it not be that criminality is merely the persistence or re-appearance of this nursery stage of development which becomes ugly and dangerous simply because of the greater strength and sophistication of the adult? After all, it is natural enough to want, to have what one desires as quickly and simply as possible, and it takes training to regard a more devious proceeding as proper. We know, too,

[1] *The Roots of Crime* (London, Imago, 1960).

that some kinds of minor criminality are frequent enough amongst quite ordinary people. May it not be, therefore, that criminality is the 'natural' condition of man and that we are all latent criminals, proof against ordinary temptations only because we have been taught to wait for what we want and to abhor the direct methods of the criminal?[2]

A certain amount of biological and ethological theory also supports the view that, as far as males at least go, aggression and acquisitiveness are innate and, from the viewpoint of the species as a whole, extremely functional for survival. We ought not, therefore, to dismiss this approach out of hand simply because it suggests that we are not entirely responsible for our actions. Moreover, psychological work done many years ago by Lange, and published in his well-known book *Crime As Destiny*, indicated that personality structure which is genetically determined can produce subsequent criminal behaviour. And quite recently no less a scholar than Professor Eysenck (*Crime and Personality*, London, 1964) has put it forward once again, adding further experimental evidence to support his view, that social deviants are genetically disposed, and that, in particular, they evidence so poor a degree of conditionability that they can never be more than imperfectly socialised. Conscience, to Eysenck, is no more than a set of conditioned reflexes. Dr Glover, whose book I have already quoted from, also denies that the conscience in the more traditional sense of the word truly regulates our actions. Glover avers that 'morality and social behaviour depend primarily on the smooth operation of unconscious codes laid down during the process of upbringing'.

We have no need to go as far as Michael Argyle,

2 *British Journal of Delinquency*, vol. I, no. 4, 1951.

lecturer in social psychology at Oxford University, does when he states that 'there is no meaningful sense in which a person who succumbs to temptation could have acted differently', and that 'it is surely inappropriate to praise and blame people in a backward-looking way for their past actions, when these could substantially have been predicted . . .'[3] This is almost to go to the limits of what Eysenck himself calls 'therapeutic nihilism', and even Argyle is not entirely pessimistic about the future, believing 'that one may use praise and blame as a means of influencing future conduct'.

I think I do not misinterpret either Eysenck or Argyle when I say that they believe that punishment for past offences is more or less a waste of time, and that the proper social aim should be concerned with reform for the future. We ought, hence, to worry less about blame and responsibility and much more about what steps can be taken to prevent a repetition of the offence. Eysenck suggests that we should first of all try to find out, on a national scale, which individual children are by birth poor conditioners, so that if they do fall foul of the law we will have an idea of the kind of treatment which is likely to be successful, and so avoid the waste of time and energy involved in applying alleged remedies which are almost certainly going to prove abortive. He suggests that drugs have much to offer us in the matter of making individuals more susceptible to conditioning, but above all he recommends immediate and urgent research in this psychogenic area of the general penological field.

My own view, for what it is worth, is that we have got to

[3] 'Delinquency and the Psychology of Morals', *The Listener*, 21 June 1962.

retain the notion of personal responsibility, otherwise there is a real danger that society itself will collapse. At the same time, we should progressively seek to eliminate the purely retributive and solely punitive element from our penal system, seeing the offender as a challenge to our ignorance more than an insult to our established order. My preference in the psychological and psychoanalytical field is more for Ian Suttie's view than for Freud's. Suttie[4] denied that a child is born with a set of instinctual drives all of which are struggling to assert themselves. Instead of Freud's idea that a conflict between love and hate springs from the child's inevitably ambivalent attitude towards its nurturing yet frustrating parents, he emphasises the child's need for a simple and secure attachment to parents as the natural growing point for the human personality. It is only when something goes wrong with this basically benign process that maladjustments occur and possibly deviant and criminal behaviour follows.

The question now arises as to what makes the process go wrong and what environmental factors interfere with the healthy growth of mind and body. If the sound person in the sound society is not at risk, it must follow that most if not all our social problems, including crime and delinquency, are socially produced and environmentally transmitted. I do not see why either assertiveness or acquisitiveness should make it inevitable that criminality results. At the most they make it more possible in a social setting which encourages them to excess, or which links them invariably to individual enterprise and adorns them with personal honours and rewards. But to say this is not to say that crime is an abnormal manifestation. It

[4] *Origins of Love and Hate*, London (1960).

is merely to say that in social conditions which in many ways foster attitudes of naked egotism and self-aggrandisement, crime is a likely by-product and, to some extent, a normal manifestation.

The most hopeful line of development, then, seems to me to lie in the direction of increasing social controls and rethinking the values which we have built into many of our established social institutions. This is a point I made earlier in this chapter, and I will now take it up again because it seems to me to be crucial for a full understanding of the complex nature of much delinquency in modern industrial societies, in which the profit motive and the institution of private enterprise and the acquisition of personal wealth are central motifs.

No discussion of the relation between crime and society, however, can avoid saying something about the family in which the primary socialisation of the child normally takes place. The close intimacies and deep emotional involvements of family life make it a potent source of psychological disturbances of various kinds, some of which may manifest themselves in the guise of delinquent behaviour. But we must also remember that the family is itself a social artefact, subject to stresses and strains generated by external pressures and influences within the wider social system. It is in disturbances of family life that delinquent tendencies begin, but it is in social experience outside the family that these susceptibilities are either developed or extinguished. The environment is always much wider than the family and its influence is constantly at work, even indeed inside the family, since the parents themselves derive their notions of how children should behave and how they should be treated from their own childish experiences and also from influences emanating from the wider cultural milieu.

Amongst the major sources of psychic disturbance within the family situation, social scientists have highlighted emotional deprivation arising from the loss of or separation from the mother or mother-substitute during the earliest years of a child's life. In normally structured families they have indicated that a lack of consistency in training and erratic disciplining are further sources of maladjustment amongst children, while, from the criminological point of view, inadequate or criminal parental models are obviously significant. Slum conditions make the job of bringing up children extremely difficult; not only are there problems of poverty and overcrowding to contend with inside the home, but there are further frequent sources of adverse social influences, e.g., groups of footloose, undisciplined juveniles in the surrounding neighbourhood, not to mention possible adult sources of delinquent contamination. Lower-class children, and boys most especially, who are by nature stubborn, uninhibited, and physically active, need particular care in unfavourable social environments, and, although it is very likely that the preponderance of children who are delinquent deriving from socially depressed areas is to some extent the result of social discrimination and our class-biassed attitudes in dealing with offenders, it is impossible to deny that there are delinquency-producing parts of big cities where hard-pressed parents need special kinds of support and guidance in the way of play centres, day nurseries, youth clubs, and various other out-of-school activities and programmes. Delinquency is, of course, often a matter of degree and marginal differences in family care and neighbourhood influences can, in the event, prove decisive.

Cyril Burt said many years ago now that 'The born criminal—*il reo nato*—is merely a pseudo-scientific myth'.[5] I largely agree with him, although this dictum does not rule out personal proclivities and constitutional tendencies which can be socially stimulated and environmentally encouraged in the direction of law-breaking and other kinds of deviance. But we would do as well to blame the criminogenic community as the temperamentally suscept-ible and constitutionally determined individual for his offences if and when he commits them. Barbara Wootton put this very forcefully:

> A highly competitive, socially hierarchical, acquisitive society offers in fact an ideal breeding ground for crimes against property; just as a mechanistic, speed-besotted age is a standing invitation to motorised violence[6].

Not only are opportunities for offences constantly increas-ing, but at the same time we are being increasingly stimulated and motivated by mass media in specific directions, many of which can lead us into breaking the ever increasing rules and regulations with which we find it necessary to hedge our public affairs around. Donald Taft, the well-known American criminologist, put it this way:

> Crime is correlated with social change. Our dynamic culture is criminogenic[7].

The problem arises not so much because we live in an affluent society, but because we live in an affluent society

5 *The Causes and Treatment of Backwardness*, London (1952).
6 *Crime and the Criminal Law*, London (1965).
7 *Criminology*, New York (1956).

which lacks any clear sense of direction and moral consensus. The dichotomy in the western world to which Professor Galbraith has drawn our attention, of 'public squalor and private affluence', is not so much an economic as a moral and political problem. We could use our wealth differently. We could afford social status for many other kinds of criteria than the acquisition of either wealth and/or power. There is all the difference in the world between the honour afforded to a multi-millionaire big business boss and that afforded to, say, the late Dr Albert Schweitzer. But there can be no doubt that our overall social structure, the social institutions sacred to business, commerce, finance, evoke a more extensive flock of active disciples than did the saint of Lambarene.

You may think that I am overdrawing the picture, that I am laying it on too thickly. Admittedly I am drawing attention to extreme situations. I am pointing to what is the ultimate logic of the social system, and I am doing this because, in our rather desperate search for the causes of crime and the sources of delinquency, we have looked in vain for cures which are based on the notion that individual psychopathology is the fundamental origin of the disturbance. In spite of the development of child guidance work, in spite of the multiplication of the social services and the initiation of ever more subtle helping agencies, crime and delinquency increase apace. The reasons for this disturbing and discouraging phenomenon is surely that we have failed to understand the nature of the basic social matrix whose influence, although implicit, is universal. If we are to understand the nature of crime we must stop looking for devils in the mind, for psychogenetic stigmata and freakish idiosyncrasies of growth, and look instead at the social situation itself and try to appreciate how the individual actors in that situation see themselves and their acts.

If you still doubt the force of what I am arguing, then may I ask you to consider yet another striking and widespread criminological phenomenon—the fact that men are much more criminal than women and boys more delinquent than girls. To quote Gresham Sykes on this topic:

Before you leap to the conclusion that man's physical nature is a source of criminality, let us note two things: (1) although most criminals are probably male, most males are probably not criminals; and (2) differences in the behaviour of men and women in our society far transcend the biological differences between the sexes . . .[8]

Sykes goes on to suggest that it is the social positions held by men and women respectively which produce this differential crime rate. He argues that, if this were the case, then

as the social status of men and women become more nearly alike, their crime rates would become more nearly alike. And, indeed, a number of comparisons bear out this line of reasoning. During the years of the Second World War women in the United States came to hold a social position more nearly like that of men, and the difference between their crime rates decreased accordingly.

A second important phenomenon, to which I have already drawn attention at the beginning of this chapter, and one which immensely complicates our efforts to treat and prevent crime, is our general ambivalence towards offenders. This is probably as much a psychological as a sociological phenomenon, but the nature of the social matrix itself is again considerably responsible for the fact

[8] *Crime and Society*, New York (1956).

130

that we as citizens have such mixed feelings about crime and deviance. In some sense it may be true to say that the presence of criminals and deviants in our midst is a psychological and sociological necessity. Emile Durkheim argued long ago that we need our criminals in order to unite us socially, and one might add that we seem to need the objective spectacle of criminals being punished in order to reassure us about the basis of our own tenuous hold on morality and legality. Those who are most vociferous in their condemnation of others and who clamour for sterner punishment are usually those who know in their own hearts that they are themselves most sorely tempted in those precise directions. We have very good evidence from the New Testament that this is so. Surely, it is the prudes afraid of their own so-called lower nature who are the most vigorous advocates of censorship and the keenest hunters of pornography!

The interest in crime is so great in contemporary society that it seems to be impossible to account for it without invoking the kind of explanation I have given above. Not only is the press filled with accounts of violence, drug addiction, criminal and delinquent conduct, immorality, and abnormalities out of all proportion to their actual incidence, but literature and the arts are similarly obsessed with the deviant and the aberrant. There is now a 'theatre of cruelty', and the novel is becoming filled with incidents which similarly epitomise man's slender hold on civilisation. One commentator has gone so far as to call the drama of crime and punishment the 'passion play of a secular society', so deep does our emotional investment in depravities and felony seem to have become. Nor is the victim of the offence always the passive recipient, as we formerly used to suppose: very often in certain kinds of crime he appears to connive in a subtle way at his own seduction. This seems to be particularly true of some individuals who are the subjects of sexual assaults.

The general upshot of what I have been trying to say is that crime is an extremely complex phenomenon indeed. Since it has so many subsidiary causes and presents so many symptoms it is most unlikely, to say the least, that we are ever going to be able to find curative or preventive measures which will deal with all its facets and manifestations simultaneously. Only a long and strenuous process of research, experimentation, and scientific analysis are going to unravel the tangled skein of socio- logical and psychological threads which combine to produce criminal behaviour and not until that has been done are we likely to make much progress in penology and methods of treatment. Feelings of relative deprivation are by definition most difficult to eradicate. The removal of competition could produce a flaccid and anaemic society unable to pay its way in the world. Our ambivalent feelings both regard to criminals and to their punishment will not easily be exorcised. The very nature of our culture often works against us. In Jackson Toby's words:

The very fact that rules have to be *learned* makes crime possible; the fact that situations of extraordinary temptation arise makes crime inevitable[9].

Even our existing penal measures may foster the very hostile and recalcitrant attitudes which they seek to combat. As Professor Radzinowicz has written:

[9] 'Criminal Motivation', *British Journal of Criminology*, vol. 2, no. 4, 1962.

[Crime] eludes the coercive reformatory hand, at one time recoiling, but only for a fresh surge forward, at another assuming subtle changes of shape and proportion: sometimes because society itself postulates new offences, or breeds new possibilities of violating its laws, or simply because the art of crime is always developing. But it still abides, a constant symptom in all societies, whatever their racial, national, social, moral, and economic condition may happen to be[10].

And yet we cannot, dare not, leave the matter there and relapse into pessimism and despair, which themselves are likely to make the general situation even worse from the criminological viewpoint. A policy of containment and gradual control and reduction seems to be forced upon us. We owe it to society to make the attempt and, in an odd sort of way, the offenders themselves have the right to be rehabilitated. Offences are often cries for help, and to do nothing may mean abandoning some of our fellows to lives of unbroken bleakness and futility. We must, therefore, press on with new measures and fresh ideas, hoping that if we study and analyse what we are doing we may make a little progress here and there and so help to keep the tide of criminality and delinquency within manageable limits. At the same time we must strive to make our society more equitable and morally healthier so that the weak are not so sorely tempted nor the stress-prone driven to the verge of criminal breakdown. This means, in a word, each one of us being responsible both for our own actions and for what in the public name is done on our behalf.

10 *In Search of Criminology*, London (1961).

8
Crime in the affluent society

Crime seems to be to modern society what poverty was to older days. It is always with us in some shape or form and most of us are at some time or another either actively or passively involved with it. Some are concerned with its detection and prevention; others with its treatment. Many of us are the objects of criminal acts while a rather smaller proportion of us actually commit offences of one sort or another. Thus crime is a universal social problem. It also seems to be more or less ineradicable. Nowadays, in spite of all the welfare services that have come into being over the past twenty years, crime and delinquency seem to be on the increase. People who care about the quality of our social life are particularly disheartened by this fact.

The fundamental problem can be put in this way. Prosperity and criminal conduct seem to increase side by side. On the basis of older arguments they should not. On the contrary, as prosperity spreads, so crime should diminish. Why doesn't this happen?

Sociological interpretations of the meaning and nature of criminality are useful here. They can go a considerable way towards resolving this apparent dilemma because

134

sociologists try to look at society as a whole. They endeav-our to analyse all behaviour into its constituent and func-tionally related parts. They see crime, in other words, not as immorality and wrong-doing, but as a specific kind of human behaviour which happens to be contrary to the law. They see that criminals are motivated by the goals pre-scribed by the culture in which they live. To them, the chief difference between the man in the dock and the man in the street is that the former has tried to realise the socially approved goals by using socially and legally disapproved methods. In this sense then criminals are in the main behaving normally, psychologically speaking, but anti-socially in the legal sense. A man who drives his car recklessly is behaving as immorally as the shoplifter, although, in our collective wisdom we manage to regard the former somehow as less culpable than the latter. This is due to emotional causes, not to reason.

The main burden of the sociological argument is that many kinds of crime are not only understandable in terms of normal psychology, but the attitudes which precipitate these sorts of offences are widespread through-out the whole of our society. The simple adage 'crime does not pay' is no longer acceptable. Unfortunately some kinds of crime do pay some people quite generous dividends. Certain risks are manifestly worth running. Well thought out robberies in the London area in recent years, for instance, have enjoyed a high degree of immunity. But obviously such naked anti-social acts are not attractive to the great majority of us. Even if we thought we could get away with the loot, not many of us, I think, would con-template committing such offences, not even for a great many dirty £5 notes. Strong taboos against such deeds are built into our personalities which make crimes like that altogether unthinkable.

But the affluent society and all it stands for does influence us much more subtly. We are, from the ethical viewpoint, more the products of our social conditioning than some of us would like to admit. Stronger and stronger pressures are being put upon all sections of the population to acquire more and more goods, more and personal possessions. We are constantly being titillated by the lure of the latest model, the new line, the contemporary style. Advertisements and advertisers call upon us with a thousand devices and myriad voices to be 'with it'. Poverty, or what may more correctly nowadays be called 'comparative' poverty, is felt as some kind of personal disgrace; inability to keep up with other people's consumer extravagances is experienced as a shameful degradation. The USA exhibits the extreme position of what we may loosely term the western culture ideal of maximal material comfort based on a commercial ethic of success achieved by almost any means. It is not without significance that in that country organised professional crime has established itself in the midst of society with all the attributes of big business and security founded upon a widespread system of graft, monopoly, and official corruptions. Donald Taft, the American social scientist, said some years ago:

American culture is, even if decreasingly, the embodiment of materialism. The dollar is dominant if not almighty. The symbol of success is still what Veblen called conspicuous consumption. Honest dollars may be preferred to dishonest dollars, but not a few unearned dollars *have* brought prestige[1].

[1] *Criminology*, New York (1956).

136

Thus it is by the criterion of success rather than of honest dealing that commercial careers are assessed. Financial speculators, though operating more often than not within the law, nevertheless epitomise the get-what-you-can-for-nothing philosophy of the pickpocket. Marshall Clinard's blistering exposure of the operation of the American black market in the last two wars, by legitimate and respectable businessmen, be it noted, not by recognised crooks and swindlers, remains the classic exposition of the business man's idea of unlimited private gain as a positive way of life[2].

Now if making money is a kind of religion for respectable honest members of society, what of those who have fallen below the level of prevailing norms? Is it any wonder that racketeering is widespread, that corruption penetrates high and low strata of society, that the law enforcement bodies are more or less powerless to stem the tide of crooked business and organised vice?

Recent disclosures in the American press relating to the confessions and evidence of the ex-gunman, Joseph Valachi, and the findings of the Senate Committee of Enquiry under the chairmanship of the late Estes Kefauver more than a decade ago, indicate that below the conventional surface of American life there boils and brews an unsavoury mass of corruption which threatens the future of an entire civilisation.

While it cannot be argued that here in Britain we have anything approaching the great material wealth, the individual freedom of action or anything like so pervasive a crime problem, a similar analysis can be applied. A number of significant scandals have blown across the

[2] *The Black Market*, New York (1952).

country like social typhoons in recent years which all testify to the thin division between the legal and the illegal, the immoral from the moral—the Brighton Police Enquiry, the Bank Rate Leakage Tribunal, the State Building Society scandal, the vote-rigging in connection with the Electrical Trades Union elections for the general secretary-ship, the Vassal case, the Profumo affair, and the boil-up over shady property investment associated with the Rachman syndicate. Not all these notorious cases involved criminal activities, but whether they did or not, they certainly revealed a very seamy and sleazy side to our society which made many people wonder. One of the things they must have wondered about was why we are so apt to make a fuss about the increase of petty theft amongst school-children and the alarm occasioned by the occasional adolescent gang foray associated with what we may generally call 'teddyboyism'. It is hard not to believe that the older generation have got it in for the younger ones, that the latter are judged by more strict and severe standards than their seniors, and that every casual peccadillo on the part of a juvenile is heavily frowned upon while much more serious crimes committed by the older generations are taken more or less for granted. Do we perhaps try to hide our own shame by drawing public attention to the misdemeanours of the rising generation?

The logic of what I have been saying is that delinquency is a widespread social phenomenon, and, far from it being confined to the mentally sick or the chronically deviant, it is for the most part thoroughly normal. We are all either actual or potential delinquents. Delinquents are not another kind of person altogether, a sort of subhuman species of degenerates and psychopaths. They are ordinary enough folk who have succumbed to temptation and, as far as juveniles go, they are youngsters who have been denied the guidance, discipline, support and affection that they so desperately need if they are to grow up into stable adult members of the community.

When I discussed shoplifting with some city-bred boys, many admitted that they knew well enough that theft was wrong, but that the desire to have things they could not afford to buy was often overwhelming. As one boy put it who had received stolen goods at cut prices from a mate: 'The bargain was so good, you couldn't resist it. Only a fool would let it go.' We must beware of underestimating the strain caused by the vision of plenty in the eyes of the boy from the poorer home and neighbourhood. An extremely well-behaved boy who was in camp with me in the country said in horror on entering the village shop and noting how unprotected every article for sale was 'Why, even honest people couldn't help stealing here'. The sight of so many desirable commodities so innocently unguarded made him feel acutely uneasy.

Mass advertising, especially on television, the enticements of open display counters in chain stores and supermarkets are part and parcel of the contemporary criminal climate. When we add to these external and physical allurements, which result from comparative prosperity, the growing publicity given to dishonesty in public life, business and finance we begin to see how to the youngster of today life offers the spectacle of an unending bonanza. Society is one vast supermarket from which lucky ones pick and buy what they fancy and the others have to take what they can get, sometimes by subterfuge and larceny.

It is this general climate of opinion, attitude and conduct which contributes incalculably to the alleged rise in the criminal statistics among young and older people. We will not undo the damage that is being done merely by appeals to individuals to behave better and to act more ethically. If we want to prevent the spread of delinquent attitudes we must go a good deal further than this. We need to look to the whole fabric of our social life and ensure that our social institutions are not working against us in this respect. If we want to have a 'good', i.e., moral, community, this means that individuals must personally strive to live better lives, but it means also that our institutional arrangements must be harmonised with our social values. The old notion that 'the nation's business is business' is a basically immoral concept. The nation's business, in my view, is to make the good life available to the greatest number of people. And not until we accept this truth are we likely to make much progress in the control and prevention of crime and delinquency.

9
Penal after-care and
the community

There are three fairly common attitudes on the part of
the members of the general public which characterise
reactions to imprisonment in particular, and to the
penal system as a whole. They are, first, an eager acceptance of the notion of retributive punishment, second, a
shamefaced distaste for the whole business, and third, an
irresponsible desire not to know the disturbing truth of
what is being enacted in their name. Most of us are to be
found in one or other of these categories, and this is one
of the reasons why penal reform makes such sluggish
progress in a country which is far from being inhumane or
sadistically inclined. Not only do most of us feel rather
ashamed of the ways in which offenders are treated and
hope that someone somewhere will do something about it.
Many of us go further and project some of our feelings of
guilt upon the people we employ to staff penal and
correctional institutions. This is because we are ambivalent
about the whole process. We want to be protected, but at
the same time we do not want to be closely associated with
the punitive end. We want prison officers just as we need
the police force, yet constantly quiz them to see if they are

abusing their power or not. In the same way many who are in favour of capital punishment would have abhorred being neighbour to the public hangman.

Such feelings as these make the operation of the penal system most extraordinarily difficult, and can sometimes place an intolerably unfair burden on the shoulders of prison staff and institutional personnel. When, as ordinary members of the public, we visit prison it is with a certain degree of inward shuddering. We resent the authoritarian atmosphere we find there, and rather wildly and emotionally, although—luckily—usually only tacitly, try to disassociate ourselves from what we think we see, and what we imagine we feel.

The truth of the matter is that, as a community, we really do not know what to do about those individuals who break the law, and we are especially adrift regarding persistent offenders. When they have served their period of incarceration and are released on licence or for good, the same emotionally tangled attitude still continues. How far ought they to be trusted? Should they get jobs when honest citizens are out of work? Is it right to give them any kind of preferential treatment just because they were foolish or wicked enough to commit whatever offences they were convicted for? And what about the dangers of contamination? Won't they have a bad influence on the other employees? Surely they'll think we're all softies and let us down again?

Some social theorists argue that this kind of reaction is not only common, but in some way necessary. Society needs its criminals in order to emphasise the social cohesion of the law-abiding section. The moral and legal norms have to be publicly upheld in order to foster that social solidarity which Emile Durkheim, for instance, regarded as the function of crime. Thus criminals are, in a rather macabre kind of way, necessary for our general social health. And, if this is so, we will never do away with crime as a human activity. Perhaps it is because it is only in recent years that we have become half-aware of this symbiotic relationship between ourselves and the criminals that we do have these irritable feelings of guilt. The growth of social science, and especially of psychological theorising, has made us conscious of this to such a degree that we cannot take refuge any more in a simple retributive and punitive philosophy. So the penal area becomes a tug-of-war ground for self-conscious reformers on the one hand and reactionary floggers and retributionists on the other, while the majority of us stand on the touchlines feeling impotent, futile, and guilty, and do nothing to assist either side.

Prison, as Merfyn Turner said, is for ever. Once a man has a record, or has 'done a stretch', he becomes a different kind of person. The prison community is, he argues, a monument to social failure. Others have pointed out that committal to prison involves a double punishment. First there is the deprivation of liberty while retained in the institution; then, on release, comes the longer and severer punishment in the form of social ostracism and suspicion. Society wills the former, but permits the latter. Yet clearly enough this second, unofficial punishment is against the spirit of the law and works to our general detriment. If men cannot live down their past follies, if children cannot be allowed to forget the offences of their immaturity, but must constantly be having them dragged up and paraded in public view, what hope is there of penal institutions or training having any long term success? Might they not just as likely have the opposite effect, making confirmed criminals out of delinquents, hardening anti-social tendencies by rousing sentiments of revenge and confirmed hostility to authority in whatsoever form it may be encountered?

Yet one of the strange things about British prisons is that they have an astonishingly high success rate. Something like 80% of those committed to prison do not offend again, although it would be only the most myopic of optimists who would ascribe this outcome to the rehabilitative experience of imprisonment. Most prisoners do not, in fact, stay long enough for any remedial treatment even to commence. Moreover, the most likely ones to reform are speedily segregated into special institutions, gaining for us, as Hugh Klare cogently argued, 'victories which are too easy while leaving ourselves with an almost impossible task with the rest[1]'.

It is with the rest, the hard-core offenders, the residual group of recidivists and repeaters, that we ought to be constantly concerned, for this is the group with whom society and the penal system have consistently and lamentably failed for so long. Several recent studies have described the typical confirmed offender for us in terms which dispose once and for all of the popular stereotype of the dangerous desperado hell-bent on a violently anti-social career. A Home Office Research Unit Report on *The Habitual Offender*[2] suggests that there are three distinct types of old lag who, in the past, were given a period of preventive detention. These were, first, the

[1] *Anatomy of Prison*, London, Hutchinson (1960).
[2] London, HMSO (1963).

regular housebreakers who seemed to have taken to crime more or less as to any other semi-skilled trade as a means of obtaining a livelihood: second came a specialised group of sex offenders and men who had committed crimes of violence: finally, there was a much bigger group of persistent thieves whose offences, for the most part, were of a comparatively petty nature. Tony Parker's Charlie Smith, *The Unknown Citizen*[3], is one of this grey legion of the lost, a man who, while still under fifty, had received sentences of imprisonment amounting to 26 years, yet whose whole series of delinquencies totalled no more than £178. The bulk of the habitual prisoners are men of this calibre; feckless, incurably irresponsible, work-shy, socially disconnected, lonely, deceitful drifters through life, obsessed with hard-luck stories, and overwhelmed with self-pity. Only rarely are they violent, aggressive, or a serious social menace. For the most part they are utter failures and misfits who have offended trivially, and whom, in a fit of desperation, the community has decided to lock up to keep out of further trouble. For such as these P.D. is a policy of despair. We ought to have infinite sympathy for them, shut off so long from the sun and openness of social life, and also, no less, for the prison officers and officials who are called on to look after them in physical conditions which must surely depress all but the most insensitive of human beings.

Amongst the dull, grey, socially disconnected battalion of recidivists is an almost helpless group of inadequates who seem to be able to manage their lives only within the discipline of an institution, or, outside prison walls, when there is somebody—wife, friend, relative, social worker—

[3] London, Hutchinson (1963).

who is prepared to act as a personal tutor and supervisor. Lacking such support, they return to a life of petty crime—sometimes within a few hours of release from prison. The value of pioneer efforts such as Norman House to this kind of ex-prisoner is obvious, but, at the moment, it is clear that similar provision is not likely to be made for the vast majority who must make do with what we may call normal after-care. There is widespread agreement that the latter is far from satisfactory, and for this reason the 1963 report of the Home Secretary's Advisory Council Sub-committee on the problem was very welcome [4]. Not only did it ventilate discontents on all sides, it made a number of recommendations which might go some way, at least, towards increasing the amount of help we give to the discharged prisoner. Moreover, by taking borstals, detention centres, and approved schools into consideration, the sub-committee attempted what is perhaps the first comprehensive survey of after-care practice and theory in this country. In its search for adequacy, however, it wisely differentiated between the needs of the various age groups, and did not attempt to recommend uniformity of method merely for the sake of bureaucratic convenience. Clearly the after-care problems of youths and children are different in kind from those of the middle-aged or elderly repeaters, and require a rather specialised approach on the part of officers appointed to deal with them.

The sub-committee began its report by re-stating the generally accepted view that what the ex-prisoner needs is 'a job, a home, and a friend' to meet his individual

[4] *The Organisation of After-Care, Report of the Advisory Council on the Treatment of Offenders*, London HMSO (1963, reprinted 1964).

requirements. But since so many lack one or more of these desiderata, social workers must attempt to make good the deficiencies. This work, they very rightly point out, demands skill and imagination of a high and somewhat rare order, and, at the very least, the community ought to ensure that those entrusted with such work receive as adequate a training as is available at present. What skills they require and what training will provide them was glibly glossed over by a bald reference to social casework, as though the latter were already a clear-cut method with a substantial body of theory to support it and a number of empirical studies to validate its claims. Nothing, of course, is further from the truth. Social caseworkers can agree on very few incontrovertible principles which are objectively assessible and not merely doctrinaire pronouncements. The Advisory Council would have been well advised to set up a further sub-committee to look into the question of what kind of social casework is appropriate to the needs of ex-prisoners and their families and what can, in fact, be done to help them. If the Home Office were merely to call in the people who at the moment 'teach' social casework at institutes and universities and leave it to them to determine the content of training and the techniques to be employed, the new army of after-care officers envisaged by the report would, in the main, find their task inordinately difficult and frustrating.

Throughout their report the sub-committee accepted that probation officers are the kind of professionals who have the know-how of treating criminals and could be the prototype of a reformed and decentralised Probation and After-care Service. This is a point I would personally query. Not that I doubt the integrity and devotion of many, indeed of most, probation officers. What I question are the theories they are 'taught' and the psychiatrically oriented techniques they are 'expected' to operate. The priests and highpriestesses of analytical psychiatry have social work training in thrall in this country. Many social workers wriggle uncomfortably under their sway, but are almost powerless to fight back. However, as Barbara Wootton pointed out, most social workers seem to be better in practice than in theory. A number of probation officers, to my knowledge, adopt an official line with the inspectorate and higher officers, while in their day to day relationship with their clients they rely on more common-sense methods. There is, in fact, an unhealthy air of chronic unreality about social casework which, I fear, the new institutes of social worker training established following the Younghusband Report are doing much to foster and thicken.

It is, of course, impossible to deal with the whole of the sub-committee's report here. What I can offer, however, are a few marginal comments and criticisms which, by and large, would support the *Memorandum of Dissent* signed by Professor Radzinowicz, Lady Inskip, and the Rev. Shirwell Price printed at the end of the main report. It is surely one of the most forceful and challenging appraisals ever added to such a document and one which will possibly, like the now famous minority report of the Royal Commission on Poverty, prove to be the more important part of the whole enquiry. The three dissenters doubted the wisdom of amalgamating after-care with probation since they feared that the former, already the 'Cinderella' of the service, would continue to play second fiddle to its better established partner. 'How', they asked, 'does the

Sub-committee propose to match this natural and inbred pull towards probation by an equally powerful impetus in the direction of after-care?' Such a duality of function at all levels, local and national, seemed to them fraught with difficulties which had been too lightly examined. The need, as the dissenters saw it, is for some body to devote itself exclusively to after-care in order that the peculiar problems associated with this admittedly complex service can be understood and dealt with adequately. The whole concept as proposed by the Sub-committee was, in effect, nothing but 'an emasculated version of that suggested by the National Association of Probation Officers and the Principal Probation Officers' Conference.' The suggestion here, rightly or wrongly, is that the Probation Service was engaged on a little empire building, a type of activity from which none of the social work agencies is ever (alas!) immune. They call, with much justification, for a Director of After-Care with effective status within the framework of the Central Council which the report envisages, and, working in close association with him a staff of inspectors charged solely with training and supervising a body of after-care officers at grass-roots level. Only in such a way could 'a scheme with some guts in it' be created, and the timid tampering with various notions of after-care which have characterised the last fifty years' penological history be cancelled and redeemed.

It is admittedly difficult for a lay member of the public to weigh the arguments advanced by either side in this dispute. It is equally difficult even for experts to be able to forecast with much confidence what will happen if either scheme is adopted. One can only say that, on balance, the arguments propounded by the minority seemed to be the

149

more cogent and to note, in passing, that the Pakenham/ Thompson Committee came to a similar conclusion when they recommended in 1961 that 'there should be a department of the Home Office devoted exclusively to after-care under a director with status equal to that of a prison commissioner'[5].

Unfortunately, we cannot leave it to the future to decide which view is correct. 'Time alone' will tell us little of comparative worth. Mistakes made now or in the near future will determine the course of action for a generation or more. All that we can be sure of is that the problems presented by after-care at both adult and adolescent level are of considerable magnitude and that, as far as the persistent offender goes, we have made little headway with the solution of the fundamental issues posed. Finding an ex-prisoner employment is not, at the moment, the major difficulty. As the Pakenham/Thompson Committee said, 'Even a severely handicapped man can get placed if he will allow somebody to sponsor him'. Settling down to the routines and freedom of ordinary life, strengthening the resolution and will of the individual to succeed in adjusting himself to the claims and responsibilities of normal citizenship—these present the most obdurate and complex problems to all rehabilitative and reformatory agencies. As an adjunct to probation, which is already deeply involved in its preventive and matrimonial work, after-care may well prove an intolerable additional burden which officers cannot effectively discharge without neglecting some other aspect of their duty. Somehow we have to create and operate a service which is not merely concerned with the

[5] *Problems of the Ex-Prisoner*, National Council of Social Service.

day-by-day discharge of professional functions, but which is also prepared for and capable of promoting and carrying out research into its own activities.

Social services of such a character hardly exist in this country. Most agencies embrace a doctrine and an associated methodology and proceed with a bare minimum of self-scrutiny. Some are even hostile towards the very idea of research, and the mere suggestion that their work is not yet perfect and that they do not know all the answers is dismissed with angry derision. I doubt myself that the Home Office has got the vision or the will to make of after-care a pioneer, research-conscious social work service. I am sure, however, that until the country and the government are ready to support such a venture the problems presented by the hard core of persistent criminals and the almost insuperable difficulties of rehabilitation of such men will remain unaltered. Research is always an uncomfortable experience. Questions are asked which we do not wish to know about, let alone have the answers for. Honest enquiry into the treatment and rehabilitation of offenders will inevitably bring research workers to the point of asking some very tricky questions about the nature of contemporary society itself. Is all the guilt on the side of the criminals? Are offenders one hundred per cent responsible for their own condition? Sooner or later the community must face up to such questions and their underlying implications.

The moment of truth must surely come when we accept the fact that there is a minority of offenders for whom no known form of treatment is in any way effective, when we acknowledge with shame and humility that we have tried a degree of punishment which proved quite ineffective, that we have offered a little charity, but that too was of no avail. There perhaps we will accept the fact that we have got to get down to the task of fundamental research, and that, although it offers no quick or easy nostrums, and may ultimately prove as abortive as retribution and moral exhortation, this is our solemn moral duty. We have to try every weapon in our armoury, not just some of them. Social science must have its turn too. Meanwhile, let us keep our charity for prison officers and the police, who bear much on our behalf and receive more kicks than thanks. The problem of crime is our problem. So too is the guilt and the shame.

Note: The Criminal Justice Act of July 1967 inaugurated a scheme for the earlier release of adult prisoners on licence, involving, for the first time in this country, a limited form of parole. The supervisory work is being carried out by the Probation Service in addition to their many other duties. In April 1968 the first of the lucky few —some $7\frac{1}{2}\%$ of the prison population only— were licensed under this system. Prisoners thus released were very closely vetted and the experiment seems to be so tightly controlled that no substantial change of policy is involved. All that it adds up to so far is that a fortunate handful of the more amenable offenders are being returned somewhat earlier to normal life than they would otherwise have been —a minor improvement in a system which still awaits a more drastic overhaul and renewal.

10
Over-paying the penalty

The quality of a nation's life may to some extent be
assessed by the way in which it treats its deviants and
misfits. If this is so, Pauline Morris's book *Prisoners and
their Families*[1] will cause further concern to all those who
are worried about the way we treat our offenders and who
cannot accept the bland and often unfounded assumptions
of our somewhat antiquated penology. The picture she
reveals shows that the consequences of punishment
frequently exceed the bounds of justice and humanity in
harming the innocent, and, in particular, the children of
convicted men. It is surely a canon of jurisprudence, in
our culture at least, that the children's teeth should not be
set on edge because their fathers have eaten sour grapes. Yet
Mrs Morris and her colleagues at PEP, in this pioneer study
of the results of imprisonment on prisoners' wives and
families, have shown that this is all too often the case, and
that by locking a man up we often cause acute misery to his
relatives and dependants.

The inquiry on which this carefully documented report
is based occupied several field workers for three years.

[1] London, Allen & Unwin (1965).

They limited their research to married prisoners over twenty-one years of age who had a further three months of their sentence to serve at the time of contact. The sample of prisoners was drawn from seventeen different prisons, stratified by class (i.e., central, regional or local), by type (i.e., open or closed), and by geographical location. Information was obtained from a total of 824 men made up of stars, recidivists, and civil offenders. In addition information was obtained from 588 wives and cohabitees. The sample was thus representative of a wide variety of offenders, and the interviews were carried out at sufficient depth to uncover most of the significant factors. The careful assessment of the data and the cautious conclusions drawn from them are typical of much contemporary British criminological research and are models of the way in which social scientists can contribute to the solution of major social problems if given the opportunity.

Perhaps the principal fact which emerges from the study is that the great majority of prisoners' families, far from living luxuriously on the proceeds of their fathers' delinquencies, exist 'in conditions of acute poverty, a fact which tends to exacerbate the other difficulties that beset them'. How far this poverty is the direct result of imprisonment and how far it is the outcome of long-term family malfunctioning it is difficult to decide. One thing we do know, however, is that the experience of grinding poverty is not the best possible basis for ultimate family reunion and eventual social rehabilitation. If the purpose of imprisonment is rehabilitative rather than retributive, we have simply got to take steps to alleviate the situation. Mrs Morris very sensibly suggests that this may be done by increasing National Assistance allowances and supplementing them by other payments for specific needs as a right rather than by leaving things as we now do to the discretion of local officers. Incidentally, it is clear that prisoners' families receive different treatment according to the part of the country in which they are living. The report reveals that these discrepancies are often of a serious nature, and show clearly that some NAB officers are going beyond their terms of reference and attempting to discriminate between deserving and undeserving families. Such a practice is intolerable in a civilised community and should be immediately stopped.

A further matter of vital importance is the need to maintain as close a link as possible between an incarcerated man and his family. Such a truism ought not to need stating, but it is clear from the information presented by Mrs Morris that here again is a field in which our practice lags grievously behind our principles. Conditions governing prison visits still smack of victorian crudity, conversations between prisoners and visitors in some prisons still being carried on through a glass partition and of very brief duration, often after a long and tiring journey. Moreover, the newly formed Prison Welfare Service, from which so much was hoped, is clearly not living up to expectations. Not only is there a shortage of welfare officers, but they are all too often obliged to carry out their interviews in public rooms. The total separation of the welfare officers from prisoners' home backgrounds is an even more serious defect of the present arrangements and inevitably tends to reinforce feelings of helplessness and isolation at both ends. Mrs Morris, in fact, is so dissatisfied with the way in which the scheme is working that she is led to challenge the fundamental assumptions on which it is based. Perhaps the new welfare officers do more harm than good, and ought to be discontinued.

The general problem of isolation and separation might be eased, of course, if prisons could be reorganised on a regional basis so that no man would be located at too great a distance from his home. Things could also be considerably improved if more visits were allowed, and if more frequent correspondence were to be sanctioned. Furthermore, experiments with limited home leave might be tested out with a selected group of prisoners. These are simple administrative changes which would involve no further expenditure, and might go a considerable way towards easing the situation if implemented. One wonders how long it will take for the Home Office to get round to undertaking such simple palliatives. Mrs Morris also has a section dealing with debtors in custody. This too makes most disquieting reading. The whole idea of locking up men who fail to meet their financial commitments does seem a little absurd as a method of coping with a minor social problem. Surely something more constructive on the lines of family casework support is required for such cases rather than the purely negative methods at present in use.

Mrs Morris's book could be called a long cool look at the prison service and at its underlying philosophy. The very restraint of her language and the objectivity of her approach may in the end do more to promote penal reform than volumes of impassioned rhetoric or polemical tracts.

11
Delinquency: the influence of social environment

In an article contributed to a pamphlet called *Delinquency and Discipline*[1], Peter Scott, the well-known psychiatrist, drew a distinction between what he called 'fringe' and 'hard core' delinquents, by which he meant those who by and large respond to ordinary disciplinary measures and those who seem to be impervious to such methods. This is a simple operational distinction which usefully divides the sheep from the goats and shows the two extremes of the delinquency scale. I have myself made use of a similar analysis, although using rather different terms, in describing my research into the illegal activities of a group of eighty boys living on the Merseyside dockland[2]. The results of this enquiry led me to distinguish between what I called the 'environmentally conditioned delinquents' on the one hand and 'emotionally maladjusted young criminals' on the other.

It is quite clear that the majority of juvenile offenders

[1] London, Councils and Education Press (1963).
[2] *Growing Up In The City*, Liverpool University Press (1954; revised edition 1964).

157

belong to the merely delinquent category and that their offences are the outcome of the promptings of the environment and the stimulation of somewhat ephemeral gangs. Sooner or later such boys shake down to the generally accepted standards of behaviour and their illegal acts become less and less frequent. Emotionally disturbed offenders, on the other hand, are more likely to persist in their delinquencies and, unless skilled help is available, to develop into more or less confirmed adult repeaters. Fortunately, the latter group is comparatively small. The vast majority of boys who are brought before the juvenile courts are fundamentally normal personalities. They have someone in their lives whom they care for and do not wish to injure and it is this affectional tie that guarantees their ultimate acceptance of the ordinary social controls. Love is, therefore, for them the basis of discipline and of final adjustment to the law. It is those less fortunate ones, conscious of being unloved and unwanted and living in an atmosphere of insecurity and anxiety, who continue to kick against the pricks and constitute over the years the hard core of offenders who present the toughest penological problem.

In this chapter we are considering the short-term environmental delinquents who commit the bulk of the offences—perhaps as much as 90% of the total. They are more of a nuisance than a menace. At the same time, if unwisely handled, even a fairly well-adjusted high-spirited boy could be turned into a social misfit. There is, therefore, a special responsibility on the shoulders of juvenile court magistrates to make sure that the treatment they prescribe does not do more harm than good to the offender. And if magistrates, teachers, and social workers are to do their job correctly they need to understand something about the background from which these delinquent children come and the forces which operate upon their developing minds during the formative years.

By and large, juvenile crime is an urban and working-class problem. This is not to claim that middle-class and higher income group children never go wrong and seldom break the law. What we can say, however, is that if and when such children do commit offences, other methods than prosecution are invoked to deal with them. On the basis of court statistics it is clear that the vast majority of those prosecuted derive from lower-income families and from homes where the principal wage-earners are mainly employed in some kind of unskilled, or semi-skilled, manual work. Crime—both juvenile and adult—is characteristic of lower-class districts. Nor is it evenly distributed even in urban working-class neighbourhoods. Heavy concentrations are found in specific localities— often referred to, following the Chicago ecological school, as 'delinquency areas', or, in recent years, 'delinquent sub-cultures'. These areas are usually located close to the commercial and business centres of big cities, or to the waterfront in seaports, and are roughly co-terminous with the older overcrowded nineteenth-century residential localities for which the term 'slum' is usually reserved. Here we find many different kinds of social problems in close association: a high proportion of mental illness, high crime and delinquency rates, and above-average figures for infant mortality, tuberculosis, child neglect, and cruelty. Here, too, the so-called 'problem families' tend to congregate. Life in these localities appears to be con-fused and disorganised. In and about the squalid streets and narrow courts, along the landings and staircases of massive blocks of tenement flats which are slowly replacing the decayed terraces, outside garish pubs and trim betting shops, in the lights of coffee bars, cafés, and chip saloons the young people gather at night to follow with an almost bored casualness the easy goals of group hedonism. But the disorganisation is often more apparent than real. Behind the confusion lies a pattern of subcultural life which has its own customs, standards of behaviour, and characteristic attitudes. Delinquency seems to be part and parcel of that established way of living or sub-culture to which the majority are obliged to conform. Petty larceny, shop-lifting, lorry-skipping, bunking into cinemas without paying, rowdiness, and occasional outbursts of physical violence flourish amongst the children of ill-regulated homes and have become almost acceptable modes of behaviour. The deviant boy in such a neighbourhood is the one who abstains from any form of delinquent act and he is likely to be penalised by ostracism and ridicule. Most normal boys conform to the pattern to some extent or another, and for shorter or longer periods indulge in illegal and forbidden acts. The years from nine to seventeen are especially vulnerable, and it is not until twenty is reached and passed that we can be fairly confident that a youngster is going to keep clear of trouble.

Delinquency in the slum sub-culture is, therefore, phasic in character. But the phase can last for ten years, and bring the boy into court on more than one occasion. It is a dangerous phase which, if things go the wrong way, can leave a lasting scar on a boy's life and a mark against his name. But the essential point we have to hold firmly on to is that, in origin, it is largely social and is a manifestation of psychological normality.

The problem from the sociological point of view is how we are to account for the existence of these subcultures. Historically there can be little doubt that they are the outcome of the gross social and economic inequalities which became so frightening a feature of British society during the period of imperial and commercial expansion in the victorian era. The workless remnants, the failures and outcasts, the misfits and unfortunates in those grim days lived lives of poverty and faced an often hopeless future in a mainly hostile world. Appalling living conditions coupled with endemic poverty and low social status over generations produced an attitude of mind at once hostile and depressed, fatalistic and careless, aggressive and inert, which formed the psychological basis of the slum personality type of former years. Its ghost walks today in the self-assertive flamboyance of the fundamentally insecure youths who have succeeded the earlier 'Teds' and who, from time to time, break out in violence and gang warfare with a ferocity that causes considerable public alarm.

The coming of the affluent society, full employment, and extensive social welfare services have changed the social structure considerably, but basically have left unaltered the old split between the 'two nations' and the two major class cultures of British society. Incomprehension and suspicion still divide the middle from the lower and un-skilled working-class people in our big modern cities. Where the one looks to the future and plans ahead, the other tends to live for the immediate enjoyment of today; where one values education and seeks academic qualifi-cations, the other tends to be suspicious of book learning and to prefer real men's work—work, that is to say, which gets the hands dirty and requires some sort of muscular effort. The difference is by and large the distinction between grammar and secondary modern school types. While few of the former find their way into juvenile court it is more common in the latter and arouses much less concern and shame when it occurs. The same would be true of other acts which offend against the typical middle-class mores, such as the acceptance of illegitimacy or cohabitation or girls getting married when they are already pregnant.

In these localities the fact that family size is usually well above the national average and that homes are cramped and physically inadequate has created a tradition for the younger residents in particular to seek their recreation and spend their leisure outside the home. There is no room for the children to play in the house and so they take to the streets. There is no tradition for parents to supervise or share their children's leisure-time activities; hence they sometimes come in contact with undesirable influences. Not all gangs or friendship clusters are delinquent, nor are the delinquent ones delinquent for most of the time they spend together. If alternatives, such as inter-street games, are available, they usually make use of them.

Being together, enjoying companionship, is more often than not the motivating force behind spontaneous juvenile groups. It is this rather than the desire for social status or economic rewards that makes the group so powerful an influence in the young slum dweller's life. If it is necessary to gain acceptance by committing some daring or forbidden act, most boys will submit themselves to such a test rather than remain in social isolation. If the locality offers no other way to show one's skill and daring than by breaking into a warehouse, exploring a shop, or trespassing on the railway, then the average boy will choose it and be prepared to follow an admired leader into such risky escapades. Much overtly criminal activity, therefore, turns out on analysis to be a substitute method of achieving legitmate ends by illegitimate means, and of releasing impulses which are otherwise denied by the physical background and structure of socially under-privileged neighbourhoods. The delinquency, in such cases, I would argue, is largely incidental, and may be regarded as a way of achieving goals which in other more favoured milieux are gained via acceptable channels.

One of the things which distinguishes the sub-cultural from the psychologically disturbed delinquent is, as I have suggested earlier, the fact that he has some genuine emotional anchorage even though the ties that hold him are somewhat slack. This is the reason why, even when he breaks the law, he tends to do so with moderation and with some regard for the feelings of others. In my group of Liverpool boys this sensitivity was strikingly revealed by the distinctions some made between stealing things from persons and taking them from institutions like shops and chain stores. The latter would not feel the loss, the former might have to make it up out of their own earnings. So, too, some boys said they would never take anything from a one-man shop, or from the elderly or infirm. It is the fact that they drew such distinctions and not precisely where they were drawn that is important. Because, in however elementary a form, they acknowledge the force of personal relations and can make ethical distinctions based upon consideration for other people's feelings, their social adjustment is not seriously in doubt.

They have not severed the social bonds or crossed that significant line which divides the merely naughty from the consciously anti-social. In the last analysis we could say that they are normal healthy boys reacting to abnormal unhealthy environmental circumstances. If this is so, then, there is every hope that we can do a lot to prevent such children ever falling foul of the law at all. The work of the Dolphin Club described in detail in a later chapter is a practical application of this kind of analysis.

Part 4

Adolescence

12
The adolescent in modern society

In the last part we considered those aspects of childhood and youth which are specifically delinquent, and we showed how, statistically speaking, the period of life between ten and twenty-one years of age is, for boys more than girls, the high water mark of crime in this country. In this and the next chapter we will look at youth in more general terms and also spend some time in examining those highly publicised but still marginal activities which are perhaps best thought of as merely deviant and near delinquent, i.e., rowdiness, rebellion against adult control, and willingness to experiment with all kinds of dangerous experiences. We will also consider the significance of one very pronounced change which has served to distinguish the present from the past generations of teenagers, that is, the emergence of pop music-making on a huge scale on the part of young people themselves. This is perhaps classically demonstrated in the rise to fame some years ago of what may well prove to be the prototype of all subsequent and successful groups, the Beatles. Anyone who seeks to understand what is going on in present day society must be concerned to a considerable extent with adolescent behaviour and must accept that pop culture of every kind has come to stay as a permanent part of the contemporary scene.

At the present time, this must not blind us to the fact that most of the changes that appear in overt adolescent behaviour are more apparent than real. Youth has always had the same needs and anxieties, but in the past resolved and expressed them somewhat differently. Moreover, most young people today are still rather tame conformists rather than Carnaby Street innovators or Soho rebels. We can, I think, to a considerable extent still say of youth *plus ça change, plus c'est la même chose*. For this reason this chapter is devoted to a general overview of youth in which the conventional and conformist elements are much in evidence. It is only when we get our wider perspective right that we will be in a position to understand the significance of the Beatles, or the Rolling Stones, or the Monkees, or to see how outlandish and comparatively less important such latterday manifestations of beatnik attitudes as evidenced in, for example, the Trogs or the flower people really are.

The first point that I would like to make about adolescence, and one that is often, I think, overlooked, is that, as a phase of human development, it is as much a sociological, as it is a physiological, or even a psychological, phase. Sociological elements are often forgotten and we tend to concentrate too much on physical and physiological factors. What I call 'social adolescence' is an indefinite period of time which continues quite a long way after physical growth has made boys and girls into men and women. But it seems to me apparent that, whatever the facts may be about the alleged earlier onset of physical maturity, young people in society today are psychologically very ready and eager to get on with their lives, and to be accepted by the older generation as responsible and mature. One indication of this, of course, is the lower age of marriage, which is one of the features of the contemporary social structure. This does seem to indicate a very strong desire on the part of the younger generation to assume full autonomy and responsibility in respect of their own affairs.

However, at the social level it cannot be disputed that the period of training, the period of further education, is getting longer every generation. More and more informations needs to be imparted, more and more skill to be acquired and transmitted, and therefore, sociologically speaking, there must be a period of social adolescence during which time this skill, this information, is imparted and acquired. This means, then, inevitably, that between childhood and full adult responsibility, there will be this interim phase when young people are perhaps psychologically fully developed but when, from the economic point of view, and from the general aspect of social status, they are still intermediate and extremely dependent upon their elders. It is this which makes the period of adolescence, from the point of view of a social scientist, particularly problematic and difficult. As far as we can judge, looking into the future, it looks very likely that this period of training and initiation will become even more protracted. Thus we can see how social demands appear to be working often against the felt needs of the young people themselves and so, one might suppose, helping to produce feelings of frustration, misunderstanding, and possibly consequent aggressiveness. This is an unpremeditated by-product, of course, of what we might call social and educational advance, and in all this change journalists and the promoters of the mass media have tended to ignore the more bread and butter aspects of adolescence because, I suppose, these aspects are, on the whole, much less colourful, much less exciting, and don't lend themselves easily to headlines.

Nowadays, I think, there is a great danger that the more mundane aspects of growing up are being completely overshadowed by the more ephemeral aspects associated with such things as rather flamboyant dress styles, colourful pop music and, possibly, a period of mild bohemianism. As we grow older, however, recreation and amusement become less and less important in our lives. The adult role begins to emerge in the later teens, centring around the fundamental task of finding a mate, securing a permanent job, not to mention subsidiary tasks such as joining a trade union, and taking some responsibility for the local, and possibly even for the wider, community.

Apart from the journalists, there are some social commentators who also have overplayed the significance of the amusement side of youth, and who claim to see a vital spontaneity of life involved in teenage culture which, in my view, is not always there. Now, undoubtedly, in the middle of the 1950s, there was a spontaneous upward movement on the part of young people, making music in a new way, and consorting together to enjoy one another's company without very much help from, or supervision by, adults. We saw, in the 1950s, the emergence of what we then called the skiffle groups, and later groups which converged on such places as the famous Cavern in Liverpool were further evidence of an unusual degree of spontaneity which all too quickly became the object of massive commercial exploitation. There is no doubt at all that there was a youthful uprising, a spontaneous growth of interest and enthusiasm at one stage, but subsequently, of course, this has hardened into a new kind of industry which has grown up in and around the beat groups and the cellar clubs. So, alas, a new kind of conformity has been born, every bit as regimented and intolerantly exclusive as any other mass movement. It may be true that teenagers today have some say as purchasers in what discs will sell most copies, and what songs are going to become the top ten or the top twenty, but this is not, in my view, the operation of a genuine adolescent cultural network. 'Pop' does not help young people to communicate at a very deep level; it merely assists, on a rather crude basis, as do clothes and hair styles, to identify a particular status group. The new interest in the so-called folk music, incidentally, appears to me to be a much more genuine form of communication, because it has some relevance to tradition, and it does seem to indicate that what one might call the hysterical phase, the beatlemania phase, is now passing.

But, of course, young people have always had obsessional kinds of interests and, in the north country anyway, the lives of the male adolescents for a very long time have been dominated by such traditional activities as football and fishing and, at the level of organising their own football teams and inter-street matches, a considerable degree of autonomy, responsibility, and initiative has been evidenced on the part of the teenage population. Some of this, in particular relation to a group of parks in the Liverpool area, I myself documented as an appendix to my

171

book *Growing Up in the City*[1]. So we must not exaggerate the importance of contemporary pop teenage culture, even though some academics have been misled about this, and with much less reason than the journalists. When my book *The Young Pretenders*[2] was published at the back-end of 1965, a Professor of Social Science in the University of Manchester wrote a highly critical review of it in *The Guardian* in which he accused me, by inference, of reflecting what he called a kind of 'worried earnestness and misunderstanding', and said that in writing about teenage society I completely missed the point of recent developments. The book was said to be like Hamlet without the Prince of Denmark, because I had deliberately avoided any detailed discussion of beat groups and pop culture. But it does seem to me that we can inflate this out of all proportion. These comparatively trivial surface phenomena are merely by-products of the comparative affluence of the rising generation, and we shouldn't exaggerate this by using rather pompous sociological terminology.

Adolescents today, in fact, many adolescents as one knows them, and as one meets them, are not nearly so confidently robust or so self-determining as some commentators would have us believe. There is the evidence, for example, in James Hemmings's[3] sensitive study of the problems facing adolescent girls which has become well known. There is also the work of new experimental advice centres for young people at places like Hampstead, for instance, which have highlighted the desire that many youngsters have for the opportunity to have a confidential

[1] Liverpool University Press (1954; revised edition 1964).
[2] London, Michael Joseph (1965).
[3] *Problems of Adolescent Girls*, London, Heinemann (1960).

172

discussion with some competent, interested, and objective third party, and Mary Morse in her recent Penguin *The Unattached*[4] makes this point again and again, drawing our attention to the essential loneliness of youth and stressing the need for the presence in their lives of more sympathetic and understanding adults. There is also the frightening fact that the suicide rate for the sixteen to twenty-one age group has about doubled in the past twenty years. Moreover, many of the young people who contributed to that publication which was called *Generation X*[5] were clearly in a mentally and emotionally disturbed condition. Some of the quotations show this very clearly—'Marriage is the only thing that really scares me'; 'You'd really hate an adult to understand you. The only thing you've got over them is the fact that you can mystify and worry them'; 'You're hell to live with, and you know it', or again:

> Morbid thoughts come and go. Parties and pop music are a good escape from descending into morbidity but, even at parties, you meet up with other young people who are searching for a meaning behind everything.

Now, that is one voice of the teenager—'Even at parties you meet up with other young people who are searching for a meaning behind everything'.

The evidence firmly points, then, to the fact that adolescence is still a period of stress and strain in contemporary society, whether we like to admit it or not, and the growing up process is far from being the idyllic, harmonious, natural developmental phase some would have us believe.

[4] Harmondsworth, Penguin (1965).
[5] London, Tandem Books (1964).

Reaction against fear and frustration can be severe—severe enough at times, I think, to merit such words as 'alienation' and even 'rebellion'. Misunderstanding and muddle and dismay are to be found on both sides of the fence dividing youth from middle-age, and, moreover, there is the very disturbing fact of human and social failure. Sufficient evidence is now available to show that the group of young people who make a conspicuous failure of their lives viewed in terms of the 'norms' of the dominant culture is substantial, and may in fact be increasing. A very careful study of a generation of boys and girls in an American mid-western town, with a population of about 45,000 people, which they call *River City*[6], estimated that 29% of the generation were educational and social failures, some of whom were showing signs of becoming permanent social outcasts and misfits. Getting on for a third of the adolescent population, no less!

We don't know precisely what the situation is in this country, though I would be very surprised not to find a similar trend observable here, even at a numerically lower level. Upward mobility for some people, of course, must mean that others get left behind. A time of general economic well-being implies a keener edge to both economic and cultural poverty for those who are left behind at the bottom of the social ladder. If opportunities to achieve and to be successful are more open than they used to be, those who do fail are all the more likely to feel rejected and unworthy, and hence be tempted to seek substitute outlets which might, in some cases, be possibly anti-social and

[6] R. G. Havighurst and others, *Growing Up In River City*, Wiley (1962).

delinquent. Thus, we see that, to the traditional psychological loneliness of adolescence, we have now added a further danger of genuine social rejection by the operation of our educational system.

But what of those who get on and achieve highly and make a success of their lives in the traditional sense of that word, who obtain jobs with good prospects and high status? There are, indeed, a great many young people who work what you might call the high school/university examination system with considerable success. Jackson and Marsden[7] have recently given us a picture of a handful of successful youngsters from a north-country town, who climbed up into the middle classes by their own exertions. Ultimately we see them becoming more bourgeois in their outlook than the established bourgeoisie. Forgetful of their own humbler origins, apt to be censorious of the lower-class culture they have recently left behind, and highly critical of the 'dim ones', as they call them, who failed in the academic rat race, this portrait by Jackson and Marsden is not an inspiring one. Nor, for that matter, is the general picture presented by Miss Veness[8], who, with the help of some of the students of Birkbeck College, carried out an enquiry into the aspirations of a group of 1,300 school leavers from all kinds of schools in two English counties. Their general attitude towards the future was one of sober hope of future contentment, the support and comfort of a well-equipped home, enough money to spend without incurring debt or anxiety, and, with the boys especially, an interesting job.

[7] *Education and the Working Class*, London, Routledge and Kegan Paul (1962).
[8] Thelma Veness, *School Leavers*, London, Methuen (1962).

The cosy domesticity of those objectives may strike a little chill to the heart of anyone who retains the more romantic concept of youth as the espouser of lost causes and as the champion of everything that is idealistic. Nothing here, in the study of school-leavers, of the great empire builders of the past, or the explorers, not a trace of a national hero. I think that our victorian ancestors would have been somewhat appalled by the narrowness of horizon displayed by most of the youngsters whom Miss Veness and her students encountered during their research. The questions that arise, which I won't attempt to answer here, are these: Is an ideology of limited success good enough for a nation which has often in the past made substantial contributions to western civilisation? And: Can a nation of pedestrians hope to maintain its position, let alone forge ahead in the van of progress, during the coming century? Edgar Friedenberg in an essay called *The Vanishing Adolescent*[9], speaking, of course, only of American youth, sounds a very pessimistic note for the future. This is what he says:

It is the fully human adolescent, the adolescent who faces life with love and defiance who has become an aberration.

'Real adolescents are vanishing', he says, and their places are being taken by tame conformists concerned only to imitate adult attitudes and to reflect established values. Thus the idea of youth as the bearer of change is nowadays becoming something of a rarity. Adolescence as a lever forcing innovation, experimentation with relationships, the creation of new institutions, is becoming a thing

[9] New York, Dell Books (1962).

of the past.* We are on the verge, perhaps, of a mediocre, meritocratic society from which excitement and danger are excluded, and where the old spirit of enterprise and hardy adventure is in decay.

Well, these are somewhat pessimistic views to which I don't entirely subscribe, but the two major problems may be put in this way. First of all, problems that arise from over-conformity and mediocrity: How shall we indeed renew the lost spirit of idealism in a world so obviously materialistic in outlook and so threatened physically by the possible outbreak of genocidal world war? And secondly, problems which arise from under-conformity for the minority: What shall we do to prevent the failures becoming socially alienated and dangerously reactive against all authority? We can, of course, exaggerate both the problematic aspects. We can fall into the common trap of ignoring the average majority by over-concern for the extremes. In between there is an enormous body of young people who manage to survive the rapids of childhood and youth more or less unscathed, and to emerge into the estuary of adulthood reasonably well adjusted to the human condition, more or less at peace with themselves and with their fellows, and able to live comparatively harmonious lives. The great merit of a recent book by the present Dean of Liverpool, the Rev Edward Patey[10], for instance, is that he

* Recent rebellions on the part of university students in various American and European countries however show that this is changing. Students at the moment are politically on the move and are producing significant social results, e.g. in France, Spain and Yugoslavia. In British universities student demonstrations are rather more petty, aimed for the most part against college disciplinary codes and methods of teaching and examining.

[10] *Young People Now*, London, scm Press (1964).

has concentrated on giving accounts of actual young people who are actively engaged, through school or church, chapel or youth group, in constructive and creative enterprises. The youngsters he described in his pages are concerned about such things as the ecumenical movement, world peace, the war on want, responsibility for the welfare of others, and notions of duty and service which make most heartening reading for anyone who has been overfed by a surfeit of delinquency, drug addiction, aimlessness, world rejection, and the restless pursuit of unending entertainment, and all the other things which some of the social scientists and journalists would have us believe to be the hallmark of contemporary adolescence.

It is equally wrong, of course, to see rebellion in every aspect of adolescence which does not slavishly repeat the paternal pattern, to produce a sort of adolescent witch-hunt mentality. Some degree of repudiation of our parents is necessary for our personal development. Originality is a benign feature of the teenage experience, it ought not always to be interpreted as deviance. But while we should be aware of creating artificial social problems out of our over-concern, it would be, I believe, a complete betrayal of trust and responsibility to abdicate altogether and leave youth to the pressures and influences of commercial exploitation and *laissez-aller* non-philosophies. But this, in fact, is what some people, the sort of people who criticised my recent book, seem to imply ought to happen. They are so frightened of indoctrination that they are willing to abandon youth to the market place. The very use of a word like *moral* sends shudders of horror up and down their spines. Of course, this wouldn't matter if it were merely a question of an academic dispute. Unfortunately,

I believe this kind of criticism, this kind of discussion, goes very deep indeed into the nature of the human condition.

The kind of criticisms that were aimed at parts of my book denote an attitude of mind which could become so permissive that it would, I believe, threaten the very foundation of our society, and, no less, the foundations of western civilisation itself. A mere rejection of traditional values and standards, the idea that everyone can do what he wants and what he likes, the thesis that guidance is presumptuous, and that the attempt to transmit moral and ethical values is nothing more nor less than arbitrary authoritarianism could, if carried to their logical conclusion, strike at the roots of our great culture, the culture which we have inherited from the Greco-Roman world and from Hebraic and Christian sources. If we do decide to follow some social scientists and other commentators, we will be leaving young people in a moral vacuum where they may pursue their goals and develop behaviour which may, again, culminate in concentration camps, in pogroms, brainwashing, and similar diabolical assaults on the citadel of humanity. Let us remember that the motto of the Hitler Youth was 'Youth shapes its own destiny'. Youth shapes its own destiny—without any attention to other sections of the population, past or future!

The resolution of our difficulties does not necessarily lie in greater stress on conformity, or in a sheepish return to orthodoxies which are clearly outmoded and no longer acceptable, and I for one have no wish to fill the air with wise saws, or to belabour the heads of the young with passionate moral entreaties similar to those found in the sort of victorian boarding school novel that I used to read as a child, so expertly practised by the late Dean Farrar in *Eric, or Little by Little*, or in *St. Winifred's or the World of School*—highly emotional moralising of a sentimental and totally unreal kind. The only sensible way to set about reducing inter-generational misunderstandings and tensions would, I believe, be to give teenagers full responsibility for running their own lives at a much earlier age than we now do. At the same time, we ought to make of the task of preparing to do a job a job in its own right. We should afford to the student and to the young apprentice a more than transitional status. The idea that 'if a job is worth paying for, it is also worth paying someone to prepare himself to do it' is one that we could usefully explore. I see no reason why students attending courses of higher education should not receive wages for their work and be subject, perhaps, and perhaps also to their great advantage, to more of the normal disciplines of employment than they are at present. My own view, for what it is worth, is that the age of adult maturity from the legal aspect should be reached by the eighteenth birthday, instead of at twenty-one, and the proposed new legislation goes a long way in this direction. We all remember how national service worked reasonably well from a starting point at eighteen, and indeed there are good psychological and sound social reasons why this should be so.

Now steps such as these, I believe, should go a very long way indeed towards reducing the period of adolescent dependence which, at the moment, is becoming dangerously protracted for social and educational reasons. It would also give us a lead in the right direction, helping older people to abandon an over-critical or patronising attitude towards youth as a kind of over-grown child.

It should help to establish a more truly egalitarian working relationship between the various age-groups, based on greater tolerance and mutual respect. If we've got to have this period of prolonged training, then let us accept it in its own right, and offer it equality with the other two periods of life, childhood and adulthood.

From what I have said, therefore, it will be clear that what we call the 'problems of youth' are indeed aspects of problems of the wider society itself, and they cannot be seen, nor can we hope to solve them, in isolation. Youth is, in fact, a part of the greater whole, and its true dignity can only be attained when this fact is generally understood, and, finally, when this is acted upon in the framing of new social policies.

Note: Since this lecture was first given the *Report of the Committee on the Age of Majority*, under the chairmanship of Mr Justice Latey, (Cmnd 3342), has recommended that the age of legal majority be lowered to eighteen for most purposes, with the notable exception of the right to vote, which was not included in its terms of reference. The government has accepted these proposals and has promised to put the necessary legislation in hand to implement them as soon as parliamentary business allows. It is also likely that they will make a timid step in the direction of granting further freedom to youth by conferring the right to vote after the attainment of their twentieth birthday.

13
Beatlemania

I have included this essay—first published in June 1964—on the social significance of the Beatles more or less intact, partly because it may be of some slight historical interest to see the reaction of one sociologist to the famous group's activities at the height of their public limelight, but also to illustrate the fact that youth is frequently a time when new ideas and new developments are thrown up more or less spontaneously. Whatever the commercial harpies have done with and through the various pop groups, there is no denying that for a while they were one, perhaps very ephemeral, manifestation of youth's creative potentiality. This native impulse to experiment and develop new ways of self-expression can also be seen, ultimately to greater social advantage, in the spontaneous growth of groups of young people dedicating part of their leisure time to new kinds of social service.

It is a notable characteristic of this generation that in many different parts of the country young people of both sexes and drawn from different occupations and educational backgrounds are committing themselves to social work and voluntary services of many sorts; that this is done with some gaiety of heart and personal pleasure; and that, above all, it represents activist youth behaving autonomously, altruistically, and, by any standards, very responsibly. Such movements as Oxfam have always had a very strong contingent of young people associated with their efforts. So, too, International Voluntary Service has for long been active both at home and abroad in acts of brotherly help, fostering understanding and communication between young people of many different countries. More recently there have grown up the Community Service Volunteers under the inspiration of Alec Dickson, and there are many other similar groups and associations which together add up to something like a spontaneous national movement by youth of no mean proportions and of a general social significance out of all relation to their numerical strength. These are the sensitive growth points of the present, the green shoots which promise much for our future social health. They comprise the benign features of the teenage phenomenon, referred to in the last chapter, which we ought to do all we can to encourage —short of smothering them with paternalistic advice or by making take-over bids to incorporate them in the establishment. Nor should they be ignored or allowed to die through sheer adult indifference and without any sort of help being offered. Some way must be found to associate the different generations in a co-operative endeavour which does not imply the domination of the young by their seniors. In other words, what parents who care for their children and seek to promote their welfare and growth have got to do is to discover how to express their love without eating them alive.

The eruption into almost world-wide publicity of the

so-called 'Mersey Sound' reveals some interesting points about contemporary society. Chief of these, perhaps, is the comparative ignorance of most responsible adults about what is going on under their very noses. How many parents, youth organisers or, for that matter, sociologists, realised the scale of young people's devotion to the new kind of music-making and the new forms of group association? We ought to have done, but even those of us who had a nodding acquaintance with cellar clubs, and knew that boys were investing large sums of money in the purchase of guitars and drums, were slow to appreciate the precise significance of what was happening. We had to wait for the television producers and the newspaper men to jolt us into awareness.

Way back in the mid-nineteen-fifties, when I was running a dockland settlement in Liverpool, the seeds of the new beat movement were sown and the first ingenuous manifestations of it were discernible. It all began with the bombshell of Bill Haley's terrific impact on teenagers with his *Rock Around the Clock*, which filled cinemas to bursting point and led to irrepressible hordes of youngsters rocking and rolling in the aisles. We were rather frightened by this phenomenon, judged it a wild craze, and hoped it would pass away. But it stuck. Rock'n' roll groups sprouted thick and fast in every large town and city. No doubt juvenile affluence and its associated independence accounted for the speed with which the movement took hold in cities as far apart culturally as New York and Moscow.

The whole thing seemed to happen without the help or guidance of official youth workers. It seemed to be entirely spontaneous, a massive welling up from below of juvenile enthusiasm and emotionalism expressing itself in wild dance and song forms. The Mersey Sound is not peculiar to that area alone, nor did it originate there. It seems to be largely fortuitous that it has become so closely associated with Liverpool.

Perhaps one reason is that there were people in that area ready and able to exploit the movement for commercial ends. Perhaps, also, there is something particularly earthy and natural about Merseyside life which gave it powerful fertilisation. Liverpool, as a seaport, is very close to the human grassroots. It has a variegated and rich local culture which stresses the group factors and harks back to Irish and Welsh separatism. Closely following the rock 'n' roll and beat group influence has recently come a revival of interest in the old ballads and folk songs, which suggests that these emanations are all in some way associated with an old and submerged tradition.

The characteristic which, in my view, has made the Beatles what they are today is not their musical talent, but their puckish personalities, their rather low-brow goonery and clowning propensities. They express an enormous *joie de vivre* wherever they go, and it is this which appeals to both old and young alike. The music they make is like that made by many another group, a lifting and collapsing wall of sound into which, as into deep-sea breakers, the audience throws itself in exhilarating enjoyment. This element of basic, physical pleasure in the immediate moment, makes them especially appealing to our uncertain, largely agnostic, and yet friendly generation of youngsters. We feel these are four nice boys having a good time and the best of luck to them! Nobody knows what tomorrow will bring, so let's all be happy together today! They epitomise, in other words, a sensible, humane reaction to the many horrifying threats that life presents us all with today, from lung cancer to the hydrogen bomb.

The Beatles are also curiously classless, in spite of their deliberate Liverpudlian intonation and pronunciation. They are typical of the new younger people of post-war Britain. Most have their roots in the working class but they are on the way up in a great variety of ways and they no longer feel ashamed of their lowly ancestry. In fact, on the contrary, they're rather proud of it and regard it as an asset. Arthur Seaton in *Saturday Night and Sunday Morning* magnificently portrays a similar kind of assured new type of male, more aggressive in his behaviour, of course, than our mop-headed musicians, but equally at ease in the world and equally associated with the good-time-while-you-can philosophy which is often too easily dismissed by moralists as the modern paganism.

There are many lessons that we could usefully derive from a study of the contemporary beat groups. The most important is that we should never under-rate youngsters' ability to apply themselves for long hours to very hard work when suitably motivated. Very few of the many groups ever achieve fame or even make a financial success of their efforts. The vast majority are dedicated amateurs following in the wake of their more famous contemporaries. And the movement is not at heart commercially oriented, although it has, of course, been taken over by business-men who are now anxiously on the look out for ensembles to follow the Beatles, the Dave Clark Five, the Searchers, the Pacemakers, the Mindbenders, the Dreamers, the Dakotas, the Undertakers, and what have you.

Secondly, those responsible for the Youth Service

should be on the look out for similar spontaneous expressions among youth which they can foster and cherish, without taking over and organising out of existence. Other kinds of emergent groups, trainspotters, jazzmen, cycle and motorbike fans, will surely be found by anyone who is alert for the signs of spontaneity and is prepared to enable youngsters to express their own impulses in creative outlets.

It is, I believe, the positive, creative aspects of the beat group culture that need to be emphasised. Whether or not the growth of these clubs and their myriad fans and supporters has reduced or is likely to reduce the amount of juvenile delinquency is still hypothetical and probably, in the last analysis, untestable. But we should not be favourably disposed to the movement merely because it might reduce crime. Obviously a great deal of surplus juvenile energy is being siphoned off into socially innocuous channels by this widespread devotion to pop music-making in young people today.

I am sure, however, that the main value we should derive from a study of the way the movement has come about is an appreciation of the deep, untapped resources which lie hidden inside young people waiting for release, resources which are all too often frustrated and dammed up by the artificial, stultifying life of big cities and conurbations, where so many are condemned to spend the best part of their lives. In testifying to the inner emotional health of youth, and illustrating the fact that the spontaneous side of human personality is by no means imprisoned for ever or without hope, the spread of these pop groups has important lessons to teach us in the fields of mental health and of education. There is a real danger, however, that this lush and healthy growth is already being distorted or even killed as a result of commercial exploitation.

Part 5

The social role of the family

14
The delinquent, his family, and the social group

It is extremely difficult to present an adequate conclusion to a book of this sort which has ranged so widely and often so speculatively over a great variety of topics and sociological material. Rather than attempt to summarise what has gone before, I want to offer as a coda two essays which, in my view, epitomise the perspectives which have been advocated throughout, and which also make positive statements and suggestions regarding the ordering of our society. In the first chapter, I try to show how the family and the youth group can be creatively harnessed to the task of preventing delinquency. In the second, I examine very briefly the relationship, as I see it, between the family and the church. Some discussion has taken place in recent months about the place of the family in modern society, with a suggestion that it can, and often does, have adverse effects upon its members. Some of these criticisms I accept, and especially, in my judgement, are we right to be concerned about the claustrophobic potentialities of the modern middle-class *small* family circle. Of course, family life, like other good things, when it goes wrong has deleterious consequences. But until it is done away with as a major social institution—and I, for one, cannot see the slightest possibility of this occurring—we must try to capitalise its good effects while perhaps seeking to minimise its disadvantages. Above all we must utilise it in our efforts to cope with serious social problems such as delinquency, poverty, and mental illness. The family, like other institutions, can be moulded to our ultimate moral and political purposes; used, that is to say, to promote the 'good' life in which all individuals come to realise their potentialities in harmony and not in conflict with others, in that human kingdom of right relationships where virtually all of us long to dwell.

The special contribution that sociologists have made to our understanding of the total delinquency process—the origin, the development, and consequently the treatment of offenders—lies in their appreciation of the significance of the social group as one of the major determinants of human behaviour. Experiences in the family circle, with the street-corner play group, in a particular class in a particular school in a particular neighbourhood, present the growing child with ideas and values that are neither innate nor entirely the product of his individual psychology. He accepts such views and attitudes uncritically and on trust as the price he willingly pays for social acceptance. The significance of this in the etiology of delinquent behaviour with its well established association with gang activities will be immediately apparent.

There is indeed something in the group experience itself that is basic to human life and thus, one would suppose, intimately related to the development of personality. We are all members of many different kinds of group, ranging from the closely-knit association of the family and the extended family to the loosely structured, more or less fortuitous, cluster of chaps round the dartboard of the local on a Friday night. This, of course, is to say no more than that man is essentially a social animal. We have known this for a very long time: the house system and the team spirit are expressions of the same fundamental tendency to work through groups. What is new, however, is the realisation in recent years of the immense therapeutic value of the group and the extent to which support in terms of fellow feeling, sympathy, and comradeship within its circle of relationships can be given to people who might otherwise break down and become mentally ill. Group psychotherapy as practised by psychiatrists at some clinics is one development of this theme, but it is likely that all group experience has a certain therapeutic value, the hockey club, and the church choir no less than the analytically oriented group under expert medical guidance.

It would seem logical to suppose that, since therapy can be achieved through group experience, the origin of many problems of behaviour and other seemingly individual difficulties may equally reside there. This, broadly speaking, is the approach favoured by many sociologists which, when combined with the understanding derived from psychiatry and abnormal psychology, offers the most hopeful perspective in all matters of crime prevention and treatment.

It is important not to make too sweeping claims for the purely sociological analysis. While an appreciation of the contribution of group cultural norms and accepted values to the etiology of delinquent behaviour will in a majority of cases be the most useful approach, there are a minority of cases where this perspective will be definitely misleading. Not all delinquency is socially induced or socially conditioned. It is equally true to say that no human behaviour can take place in a complete social vacuum. The two insights—psychiatric and sociological—reinforce and complement each other, and the balance in different cases will favour one aspect or the other but seldom if ever to the complete exclusion of either.

There emerges, then, the possibility of utilising people's natural desire to be together and to do things in company as a therapeutic technique for coping with their various problems. The psychotherapeutic group approach employing psychoanalytical methods has apparently been found to be effective with patients suffering from certain kinds of neurosis and other personality disorders. Experiments have also been made for a good many years now with what might be termed environmental group therapy involving the establishment of specialised communities, guarded against certain dangerous situations but nevertheless free enough to permit conflict and aggressive outlets necessary as a preliminary step in the process of the social re-education of problem children and delinquents. The influence of August Aichhorn is far-reaching in this field, and there have been interesting accounts of similar experiments with delinquents and maladjusted children living in controlled environments, on the far side of the Atlantic by Bruno Bettelheim and Fritz Redl and in this country by David Wills. The communities described in these studies are not only psychoanalytically based to a large extent but they exist apart from the ordinary life of the general community. Social group therapy of the kind to be discussed in this chapter, although it may make use of psychoanalytical insights, is not primarily concerned with cases of psychiatric breakdown, and is moreover, even when it involves the creation of a new social institution, closely linked to the ordinary life of the neighbourhood and community very much in the same sort of way that a school is. The institution will be more like a club, that is, than a clinic. The children who attend such organisations are not thought of and certainly are not treated as individuals apart from their home base or without reference to their general social environment. They are members rather than patients, participants who share in the creation of a pattern of relationships and activities in which they find some pleasure, some degree of emotional release and personal reassurance.

The concept of the 'transitional community' is perhaps most apt for a description of the therapeutic social group. Such a group as I will shortly describe, concerned with the socialisation of juvenile delinquents, may be thought of as providing a bridge between family life and the wider community and the leaders or workers engaged therein as parent-supplements and surrogates providing that degree of affection, interest, or discipline that the children's proper parents may not be able or may have refused to provide. Many problems of delinquency and other behaviour disorders are rooted in the home and spring from faulty family relationships. The social therapeutic group provides some of the things that the more basic group, the family, has failed to provide; a new group is called into being, as it were, to redress the deficiencies caused by the failure of an earlier, primary group situation.

Social groupwork appears to operate at two different and distinct levels, one consciously planned, the other resulting from the operation of natural forces in the group situation. Merely by bringing people (in this case delinquent children) together, certain natural therapeutic agents are released which assist the skilled leader to promote the positive values, goals, and attitudes which are deemed socially desirable and individually beneficial. This is usually more effective than mere exhortation or any resort to threats and punishment. The fact that the beliefs and values of the individual are deeply grounded in the life of the group or groups to which he belongs must be kept constantly in mind by the groupworker in all his efforts to change behaviour and attitudes. He strives to create a new, small group, a part of—yet, in some ways, very distinct from—the rest of the community (but not thought of by the members as being in any way abnormal!) where the norms approximate, or can be got to approximate, to the goals and values he is seeking to promote amongst the members. In order to get children to attend such a group, and perhaps to drop some of their streetcorner associates, the worker must offer some sort of inducement to overcome the initial resistance. Naturally enough this is a most difficult phase, and it is not always found possible to get delinquent children safely over this first step. In the experiment I am going to describe, certain pressures such as parental persuasion or the guidance of probation officers were made use of to ease reluctant children into the group. Once there it had to be left to the attractive nature of the programme and the warmth of attachments built up either with the adults or the other juveniles to recondition attitudes and modify relationships.

The programme should be so arranged that it provides controlled outlets for the urges and impulses that hitherto have found expression in delinquent escapades. For one thing there must be a degree of excitement and adventure, even of danger, from time to time, so that the youngsters may prove themselves to themselves and to their associates. By proving themselves, I mean undertaking some activity which brings them into the limelight, involves courage and skill, and, if carried to a successful conclusion, confers prestige. It is vital, therefore, that the programme should offer opportunity for the display of physical prowess for the tougher boys, yet, in order that the more timid ones should not be further frightened, it must be of an optional nature and something that can, if necessary, be avoided. Boxing, football, certain kinds of physical recreation of an obstacle race kind, and, above all, camping out and similar expeditions should share the programme with the more artistic and technical pursuits through which the child gains poise, and a chance to be quietly watchful, reserved without withdrawal, and to shine in a less dramatic and physical way.

The Dolphin Club, a boys' club with a difference, was an attempt to provide a therapeutic social group with the purpose of preventing and treating delinquency in a central urban environment. While incorporating some of the traditional club methods in its organisation it had to go a good deal further than the orthodox youth organisation and develop other techniques appropriate to its main objective. The age of admission to the Dolphin Club was fixed at the age of criminal responsibility, and it left off at a time when boys are usually admitted to the ordinary youth organisations, round about the thirteenth or fourteenth birthday. By the time a boy had spent five years or less in the Dolphin it was hoped that his behaviour would have so improved and his personality been sufficiently socialised for immediate transference to a club for older boys and adolescents operating, in this case, in the same building and drawing its clientele from the same locality. The members were divisible into two main groups, the 'problem' boys and the 'easies'. The problem boys were further divisible into those who were known to be delinquent as defined by a court appearance and conviction, those who were known to be minor, unofficial, or undetected offenders, and finally those boys who were emotionally disturbed. These groups overlapped in some cases: in particular there were boys who were delinquents and who were at the same time disturbed. Most of the members were sponsored, by which is meant they were introduced to the club by parents, other relatives, school teachers, or social workers. Twenty-eight per cent of the total intake were introduced by probation officers and about half this number were brought in by school teachers. Only a small proportion, five boys in fact, were brought by their own parents. This is itself an eloquent commentary on the general parental attitude. The system of sponsorship was more than a mere recruiting device. It gave the club a further hold on the boy and an additional lever to bring pressure to bear either on the children or the parents. The scheme worked particularly well with probation officers and juvenile liaison officers of the city police, but much less effectively for those cases sponsored by parents or other members of the kin-group.

The Dolphin needed to be much more authoritative in

its internal leadership than is advisable in the adolescent group, partly because the younger boys had less solidarity, a less developed social conscience, than older boys, and partly too to provide for those who lacked a reliable and consistent home discipline (perhaps as a result of the death, desertion, or absence of the father), a measure of security necessary for their emotional stability. The group was purposely kept small, with a maximum of forty and a median membership of thirty, so that leader- and helper-member relationships could be as intimate and sustained as possible. Very often it was found that a boy maintained his association with the club on account of his happy personal relationship with the leader or with some other adult worker and that this, rather than the attraction of the various activities or the pull of friendship with other boys, proved to be decisive for overcoming the power of delinquent associations and in promoting satisfactory social adjustment.

The club was opened every weeknight evening for a period of two to two and a half hours, while, during the summer, outdoor excursions, trips, and camps were organised at weekends. Members were expected to attend every session and regularity of attendance was stressed when initially negotiating with parents and written into the rules of the club. In the event of absence the full-time leader in charge of the group would usually make an immediate visit to the home to discover what had happened to the absentee. This was done partly to prevent parents being misled into thinking their children were safe in the club when they were in fact roaming the markets or the city streets, and partly to bring home to parents the seriousness of the club's purpose and the extent to which the workers were prepared to go to assist them in safeguarding their children from criminal influences. Regular and efficient home visiting was in fact the kingpin in the whole of the Dolphin organisation. No boy was accepted into membership without a request from the parent or parents followed by their promise to see that the child attended regularly and arrived back home again within reasonable time. The club, as it were, entered into a form of partnership with the home, undertaking to carry out certain agreed duties concerning the leisure-time activities of youngsters in return for which the parents undertook to collaborate by sending their children regularly, by encouraging them to take part in the whole programme, and by notifying the workers of unavoidable absences and consulting them should any problems related to the children arise.

From time to time a very limited amount of financial assistance might be given to families in particular need, for example to equip a boy to attend a camp or to go on an expedition; there might also be small gifts of clothing, or more usually loans. Parents were encouraged to seek out the club workers for advice, and many of them did indeed consult them on the problems their children were presenting. Conversely, the workers could at times take the ball into their opponents' half by giving advice unasked to parents who appeared to them to be failing in their duty, or who did not seem to understand the importance of their attitudes in dealing with their children. One father, for instance, was castigated for not expressing and showing in action the affection he said he held for his boy. A mother was given advice about consistent disciplinary treatment and warned of the consequences of alternating between extreme severity and leniency. More than once a father had to be cautioned against using physical punishment or a mother against voicing threats of 'having a boy put away'. At such times the workers went to some pains to explain how such parental attitudes intensified the problems which they with the parents were jointly engaged upon solving. A good deal of parental education and advice on handling children was given which was occasionally resented and produced a hostile reaction. Usually the home visits went off smoothly because in fact, in spite of bewilderment, ignorance, and fear, the majority of the mothers with whom the club workers came into contact were genuinely concerned about the welfare of their children and eager to do what they could to help. This co-operative relationship underlay what earlier in this article was termed acting as 'parent-supplements'.

I say 'mothers' advisedly, for although the club had contact with a number of fathers it was the women of the household with whom for the most part the workers found themselves dealing. The lack of male support in many of the homes from which members derived was one of the noteworthy features of the experiment. Out of a total of sixty-six households there were thirty-one cases where the fathers were not able to carry out their complete responsibilities owing to working out of the city, desertion of the home, death, divorce, legal separation, or chronic invalidism. By contrast, in only two cases were the women not making some effort to fulfil their responsibilities. The fact that nearly half the households lacked a firm, stable male leader is more than likely to have had a significant bearing on the behaviour of the children, particularly the boys, as hey approached adolescence, and the evidence suggests a possible connection between delinquency proneness in the sort of subculture where the Dolphin Club operated and the absence or ineffectiveness of the father-figure round about the time boys tend to want to break away from maternal dependence. Hence, the extreme importance of the club leader and adult helpers in assisting the boy in the capacity of father-figures and parent-supplements during this particular phase. The importance of the male role in child development has in recent years tended to be somewhat obscured by concentrating attention exclusively on the mother-child relationship, and is a topic that is likely to receive more notice as our researches into delinquency become more sensitive to the significance of differential parental roles in family life.

It will be clear by now that the Dolphin experiment as a piece of 'action research' went rather further than merely providing group experience and recreational activity for a number of difficult boys. A good deal of time and attention was given to individual members and to contact with individual families, and as the project developed the workers found themselves moving towards a service which would incorporate vital aspects of both groupwork and casework techniques within the same group framework. No effort was made to undertake what may be termed 'deep casework' either with parents or children, and the idea of psychoanalytical methods or treatment was at no time envisaged. The sort of casework practised by the club workers was largely that of the old-fashioned and well-established kind universally undertaken by such people as probation officers who, although in attempting to understand an individual's behaviour might make use of psychiatric insights, are not qualified to make use of kindred techniques at a treatment or therapeutic level. The novelty of the Dolphin Club lay, therefore, on the one hand in the efforts made to overcome most of the usual objections to the more traditional types of boys' clubs, such as danger of excess numbers and consequent contamination, tackling children at too late a date, and on the other hand in the strenuous endeavour made to establish creative relationships with fathers and mothers in the bond of a two-sided working partnership.

The membership of the club contained a high proportion of boys with behavioural problems; many of them were actually and most of them potentially delinquent. This group, fifty-five strong, formed the kernel of the experiment, and it was upon success or failure with this type of member that the value of the club as a method of delinquency prevention and treatment depended. Forty-seven of these 'problem' boys were ascertained to be delinquents, while the remainder were clearly psychologically disturbed. As might be expected with such a problem-saturated group, there were numerous failures—judging success by whether a boy was retained in membership for a reasonable period of time, and showed indications of improved behaviour, (i.e., less delinquency or less strained personal relationships), and judging failure by the loss of boys, deterioration in behaviour, and, in some cases, committal to approved schools or other residential institutions. Some of the severely delinquent boys were received too late into membership and their delinquent habits too deeply ingrained for the club workers to achieve any remedial result. Other children received so little support from their parents that most of the workers' efforts were neutralised and made ineffective. On the whole the club seemed to be least effective with those boys who came into membership after already having been convicted of one or more offences. Only six out of the twenty-eight boys in this category were successfully retained.

Fourteen of the boys categorised as 'disturbed' (i.e., exhibiting signs of emotional maladjustment) were delinquent, while eight were non-delinquent. The groupwork-casework methods were reasonably successful with these emotionally disturbed non-delinquents, and the permissive atmosphere of the club and the intimate and sustained affection of the club leaders and helpers seemed to provide a measure of reassurance that was obviously therapeutic. Ten 'disturbed' members, five delinquents and five non-delinquents, were retained in successful membership.

Antony, an anxious, neurotic child who was one of the non-delinquents, responded well to individual attention and interest. Sometimes he behaved quite hysterically, losing all self-control and wildly screaming and throwing himself about the room, but face to face with a sympathetic and understanding adult he could maintain his even keel and behave in a thoroughly normal manner. An indication of his growing confidence was revealed when the club workers succeeded in getting him to go to a cinema and sit through the entire performance without fear or panic almost for the first time in his life. Antony needed constant attention, a measure of shielding within the group. In the hurly-burly of the orthodox youth organisation he would very likely have become much worse.

Apart from the delinquents and the disturbed members, the club possessed a group of benign boys who were comparatively easy to handle and who, though being to some extent delinquent risks in a crimino-genic environment, were not in any desperate need of the club's ministrations. There were thirty-six non-problem members, of whom only nineteen were successes. The majority of this group who left for unsatisfactory reasons did so as a result of parental indifferences and laziness.

Total Number of Problem or Difficult Members

Delinquents	46	
Non-delinquents	8	54
Total number of apparently undisturbed, non-problem members		34
		88

Analysis of First Three Years

Problem Cases	Failures no.	%	Successes no.	%	All Members no.	%
Delinquents:						
Official	21	72	8	28	28	100
Unofficial	6 ⎱		11 ⎱		17 ⎱	100
Non-delinquents:	⎰ 9	36	⎰ 16	64	⎰ 25	
disturbed or	3 ⎰		5 ⎰		8 ⎰	
problem cases						
All problem cases	30	56	24	44	54	100
Non-problem cases	19	56	15	44	34	100
All members	49	56	39	44	88	100

The significant fact about these statistics is that the failure rate for the problem and for the non-problem boys is the same, almost certainly a reflection of the fact that special care and attention was given to the difficult cases in terms of intensity of home contact and of sympathetic handling in the club itself. At the same time, a significant difference can be noticed between the high failure rate for official or convicted delinquents and the high success rate for the unofficial delinquents and the non-delinquent members. Insofar as it is possible adequately to assess the work of a club like the Dolphin in statistical terms at all, and allowing for the fact that failure as a club member does not necessarily imply further deterioration any more than sustained attendance at club precludes the possibility of further lapse in the future, it seems reasonable to say that the club's efforts were more successful with boys who were early or minor delinquents, but that, on the other hand, even with the more severe delinquents the chances of being able to help them seemed to depend to some extent upon the degree of parental support and co-operation obtained.

There is nothing particularly unexpected or remarkable about the results of this experiment. Nor is it always easy to say exactly why a particular boy benefited or appeared to benefit from the methods employed. Were there time and space one would wish at this stage to have a look at the records of particular individuals and try to trace out the subtle ways in which habits were changed and attitudes modified. Two case histories selected from the group of successful members will have to suffice but they may in part illustrate how the casework-groupwork technique worked out in actual daily practice.

Randy was one of the earliest members of the Dolphin,

and after four years he was successfully carried through without major disaster until he was old enough and stable enough to join the senior branch of the organisation. He was an intelligent boy but severely handicapped by an unfortunate family background, the father having deserted while he was an infant and his mother having re-married. Randy had four half-brothers to compete for the affection of his mother, and as a result of this competition and the sense of his own difference and possible inferiority, he lived in constant dread of being finally abandoned. Emotionally insecure, he not unnaturally sought compensations outside the home, and quickly rallied to his leadership a gang of younger children whom he was clever enough to be able to coerce into accompanying him on a series of delinquent activities, involving several breaking and entering offences and many larcenies. Randy found adjustment through the club a long and difficult business. Twice he was in court, and twice the club leader was able to support him through this crisis; with the help of his probation officer, strenuous efforts were made to save him from being sent to an approved school. Randy's gang were not members of the club, with the result that he was somewhat isolated with no one to boss and no one to obey him. His behaviour was generally aggressive, egocentric, and exhibitionist. He sought attention through ill temper and various forms of provocation. The club workers made a special fuss of him whenever possible, giving him privileges and presents and refusing to be put off by any aspect of his behaviour. This treatment proved ultimately effective. He responded to the adults, made personal friends of some of them, and found through constant and close association father and mother figures to whom he could relate with confidence and affection. As time went on he became more sociable, less isolated in the group, and made overtures of friendship to other boys. Perhaps the best indication of his maturing could be seen in his increased ability to suffer mild frustration and to accept minor disciplinary action.

The features of special interest in Randy's case were the intensive individual and compensatory attention he received, coupled with the gradual easing into a group situation where he ultimately stimulated less hostility. Without the group's existence and the presence of other boys to whom he could relate, the individual attention and affection might have been wasted when the moment of parting, that is to say, of growing up and passing on into a senior group, came. Equally the impact of the group in a raw situation without personal support and adult interest might have made him even more of an outsider and delinquent than his experiences with his street-corner association.

Charlie Hands, unlike Randy, was never socially isolated in the club. A tough urchin type of boy, hands and knees dirty, clothes torn, hair all over the place, he alternated between surliness and friendliness, between aggressive hostility when he hated the world and all in it, and sunny cheeriness when he was happy to co-operate with all and sundry. His home situation was largely responsible for these conflicting attitudes which mirrored his inner emotional problems. His mother had no control over him and her only technique was either to ignore him altogether or to use bribery. His father neglected him, and only interfered when personally irritated, when his only form of discipline was to use his belt and give the boy a severe thrashing. Charlie's attitude to his father consisted of blind hatred and secret emulation. He became a shoplifter in the manner and tradition of the neighbourhood, always in the company of other boys, and as a result he acquired a bad reputation in the district, and many parents tried to prevent their children associating with him. When he got into trouble and appeared in court the club workers stood solidly beside him, not condoning his offence but making it plain that they did not repudiate him as a person in any way. Slowly Charlie gained confidence and became much less aggressive. The actual club programme assisted him in many ways. He was a solid, muscular type, and he was able to excel in games and sports and display his prowess and reap the reward of prestige and captaincy. He had his lapses, times when, probably because of some trouble at home, he swore at the workers, attacked other boys, and generally took it out of the world and society. Consistent handling and firm but sympathetic and, above all, forgiving discipline saw him safely through these regressive periods until at the end of his club career he became a pillar of law and order, and actively associated himself with the ethos and many of the goals of the club. He learned to control his strong feelings, to accept rules for the sake of ultimate pleasures, and he found, too, one suspects, support in the constant relationship with the male workers to strengthen himself in his relationship with his father. In his case, as opposed to Randy's, the actual group experience, the give and take of organised life, and the outlets made available for the safe release of basic urges provided the most important key to his eventual social adjustment and avoidance of crime.

The logic of the Dolphin experiment is that efforts to assist families to discharge their responsibilities more effectively are well worth while. If in certain instances delinquency is partly the result of ineffective family relationships, it is well worth while spending time, money, and effort in offering realistic sympathy and services which may help the family over a phase of particular danger to boys approaching puberty. Boys who live and grow up in neighbourhoods where there is a strong delinquent tradition are in particular danger at this time, and need all the help that society can muster to see them over the hurdle of the dangerous years. Where home life is inadequate and the environment is criminogenic a special effort is demanded. New agencies of a character similar to the Dolphin Club have a contribution to make to any large-scale social programme designed to prevent juvenile delinquency*. The methods used in running the club are not entirely novel, nor are they likely to be successful with all problem children. Delinquency has a variety of symptoms and arises from a multiplicity of complex interrelated causes. It is reasonable, therefore, for us to equip ourselves with a variety of palliatives and a wide choice of remedies, one of which is the type of specialised boys' club and transitional community between childhood and maturity, between the home and the wider community, epitomised in the Dolphin experiment.

* See in this connection *Children In Trouble* (Cmnd 3601), April 1968, and its suggestions for 'intermediate forms of treatment' for younger delinquents which in many ways are akin to the methods used in the Dolphin Club.

15
The church, the family, and the home

If we could trace back the origins and unearth the causes of the majority of our social problems we would certainly find that we would be led to examine the quality of home life and the strength of family affection. It is in the family, more particularly in the parent-child and husband-wife relationships, that most of the problems and difficulties that reveal themselves both in childhood and in later life have their roots. These problems are manifold and universal and are not confined to any one socio-economic group or class. Divorce destroys the fabric of the family life of rich and poor alike. Healthy, well-nourished children can be emotionally starved. Criminals and delinquents are to be met in every walk of life, in the university, the new housing estate, the good residential neighbourhood as well as in the slums.

If we are ever going to be able to deal effectively with these social and ethical problems we must begin with family life and the care of children at the earliest possible stage. The hope of prevention lies in the ability of social and educational workers to get in to the family situation before serious breakdown occurs and before wrong attitudes are established and unethical behaviour has gained a firm hold on the rising generation.

The family is the primary and most important of all social institutions. It has more than one task to perform, for it is not only concerned with generation and breeding offspring but—and this is much more important—it is the transmitter of all our cultural and ethical values and standards of behaviour. What the child learns, first at its mother's breast and later in the loving discipline of the family circle, determines to a great extent what sort of a person and what type of a citizen it will ultimately become.

There is a body of convincing psychological evidence to indicate that the early years of life—some psychologists would even narrow this down to the first five years of existence—substantially determine our characters, and that what happens to us, or fails to happen to us, in infancy and childhood largely shapes our destiny for the whole of our days. This is a sobering thought, and one wonders if it is sufficiently appreciated by those who enter matrimony so lightheartedly and aspire to parenthood so carelessly. Family life not only moulds our characters and forms our habits. It is probably the most vital factor in determining mental health. For children who are emotionally deprived become problem children; the offspring of affectionless personalities are themselves likely to be affectionless, and the chronic delinquent or the chronic neurotic is frequently the result of emotional failure during his early and most helpless, formative years of childhood. Thus we see today a vast army of social workers whose job is to deal with other people's children or the products and members of families that have broken down under some intolerable emotional stress, and whose personalities have not been strong enough to cope with the strains imposed by living in this anxiety-ridden twentieth century.

We have heard a good deal in the past few years about a national breakdown in family life. A minority, but quite a substantial minority, seek a way out of their difficulties through divorce or separation orders. Others continue to co-habit in an atmosphere torn by quarrelling and poisoned by bitterness. In such a mental climate the children can hardly fail to be emotionally injured and their anxieties may easily reveal themselves in illegal behaviour and crime. It is a sad paradox and commentary on our allegedly christian community that the children who are unloved and rejected by their parents are treated as criminals and branded for the remainder of their lives as misfits and problems, when their only sin has been that their parents were incapable of loving them and that the community could devise no saner, juster way of dealing with them.

It is easy to wax emotional on this matter of the failure of many people to sustain their marriage and to keep their homes intact. Professor Titmuss has rightly drawn our attention to the fact that most of the marriages that have resulted in divorce during the past decade or so were contracted during the nineteen thirties and not under conditions of the post-war 'Welfare State', and are the aftermath of unemployment and economic depression rather than, as is so often argued, an irresponsible exploitation of an overprotective society. He has also very shrewdly pointed out that 'divorce is not a cause of family breakdown; it is a symptom.' The mere perpetuation of an external, legal relationship does not guarantee marital harmony or secure for the children a happier psychological environment than the 'broken home' in which there remains one parent who loves and cares for the offspring. If we are ever to do anything to improve family life or to 'save the home' we must go much deeper than this and offer real help and guidance so that men and women, and even unmarried boys and girls, may have insight into their own personality problems and knowledge of what marriage demands of them and what it entails in terms of self-sacrifice, mutual adjustment, and intelligent planning. Bringing up a family, mentally and physically healthy and reasonably well educated, is a task of the greatest national importance, but it is no easy business.

Developments in the field of nutrition, in medicine, in psychology during the past few years have helped to make parents more aware of these difficulties. We all remember the small boy who when being lectured by his father for a bad school report looked up at him gravely and asked, 'Daddy, is my failure due to heredity or to environment?' But, joking apart, there is a very real danger of the modern child becoming, in Professor Titmuss' words ,'the central emotional focus of the small family . . .' and 'the victim of socially induced anxiety'. Handling children, our own or other people's, requires skill and intelligence. Problems arise from lack of affection and from neglect; they arise equally from over-protection and coddling. The need is for love, but affection alone will not be an infallible guide to training children. There is a place for discipline, provided that discipline is based on genuine affection and intelligent understanding of the situation.

Several speakers and writers have suggested that the

growth of the 'Welfare State' and the development of a multiplicity of social and educational services and agencies has tended to undermine the responsibility of parents for the ordering of their family lives. So much, it is argued, is done for people that they are becoming less and less anxious to do things for themselves. A mentality of spineless dependence has resulted, with a consequent deterioration of parental standards and responsibilities. This is something that is not yet open to proof or refutation. But whether the complaint be true or not, we must accept the 'Welfare State' as a fact and develop our social planning in relation to that fact. My own opinion, for what it is worth—and this is a sphere where only personal opinions can be given—is that those parents who love their children are just as concerned and responsible as they ever were and that, however much help they receive from statutory authorities, they will go on being concerned about them in the right sort of way, while those who were affectionless and irresponsible appear to be on the increase merely because our method of diagnosis and our schemes for detection have tended to limelight their deficiencies. Even though we have created for ourselves something that may not be unfairly called a 'Welfare State' that does not mean that social problems have ceased to exist. Societies in transition constantly create for themselves fresh problems, and the very dynamics that destroy inertia cause frictions and anxieties. There are still many children in need, there are still many families in distress, there are still many people who are mentally ill. Ignorance is still the great enemy, a giant who stands deeply entrenched on our road to social security and personal well-being.

What can be done to help? What services are still needed

to supplement the services offered by our planned welfare state? What place has the church in all this, and what can church members do in this matter of safeguarding home life and ensuring that the children of all families get off to a good psychological and physical start in life? I am going to suggest one or two things that could be done immediately, jobs that are well within the scope of existing institutions and that can be placed fairly and squarely upon the shoulders of responsible adults in their capacities as citizens and church members.

In the first place there is a tremendous need for marriage training in the widest sense of the words. Our efforts in this quarter hitherto have been too sporadic, too fragmentary, too uncoordinated. What is wanted is a carefully planned, nationwide programme aimed at preparing young people for the business of married life, allied to guidance service during marriage if and when problems arise. At the present time it is widely believed that anybody can be a parent. It requires no training. It is a skill supplied by nature or intuition, or mysteriously conferred on happy couples at the ceremony before the altar or in the registry office. You follow what Mum and Dad did if you were a happy child; if not, you reverse the technique and rely on a slice of luck to see you through.

Of course, we should teach young people that marriage and parenthood are to be enjoyed, that they supply some of the deepest satisfactions of our human nature. At the same time we should make it crystal clear that this task requires hard work, forethought, planning, and sacrifice. The planning and work aspects of marriage could very well be tackled in schools as a part of any sound secondary education more useful to the community than Latin declensions or French irregular verbs. At school they could learn a great deal about housecraft, boy and girl side by side in mixed classes, budgeting, menu-planning, finding out ways of doing odd jobs and internal decoration, and a host of other invaluable skills besides. It seems to me that churches and youth organisations have an equal opportunity to do something constructive in this field at a time when adolescents are thinking seriously but not specifically about marriage and the future.

When the time comes for young people to join their partners in public betrothal a great deal more guidance should be given beyond the few conventional words from father or mother's sentimental applause. Marriage is a social institution of first importance and society has the right to expect that those who wed do so with full knowledge of their responsibilities and obligations to one another, to the community, and to their unborn children. The churches could go much further than they often do in their relationship with young married couples and with the families of those who have been united beneath their roofs. It is always possible to insist on discussion and preparation before the ceremony, and there is no valid objection to maintaining contact afterwards. If this were more generally practised much good might result, and failure to seize this opportunity is a grave dereliction of duty.

Even if and when a sound, universal scheme for preparation for married and family life is instituted through schools and churches and youth organisations, we will not be at the end of our social responsibility. There is always the family that meets difficulty, either economic or psychological, to be helped and befriended. One of the most important services is that provided by family casework agencies, most of which are voluntarily staffed and maintained. We need a great expansion of such agencies in the near future, agencies that can bring swift and sympathetic aid to families in distress and prevent breakdown and resulting unhappiness for the children. All this is social work and in the broad meaning of the words, the church's work. Christianity, as I see it, is a social religion, and not a form of private piety or a purely self-centred devotionalism. One aspect of this would be for the churches to bend their energies and deliberations to the task of defining such problems more realistically, and to devising ways in which the impulse of good neighbourliness can express itself more usefully by helping to create that quality of happy home life upon which so much depends in the future.

Reading list

This list does not include every book or article mentioned in the text but gives a selection of books which the general reader and the ordinary student might find useful if they wish to follow up some of the topics raised in the various chapters.

Child Care

DENNEY, A. H., *Children In Need*, London, SCM Press (1966).

—— (ed.), *Children At Risk*, London, Church of England Board of Education (1968).

MAYS, J. B., *Adventure In Play*, Liverpool Council of Social Service (1957).

NEWSON, J. and E., *Patterns of Infant Care*, Harmondsworth, Penguin Books (1965).

PRINGLE, M. KELLMER (ed.), *Investment in Children*, London, Longmans (1965).

Colour

PATTERSON, SHEILA, *Dark Strangers: A Study of West Indians in London*, Harmondsworth, Penguin Books (1965).

RICHMOND, A. H., *The Colour Problem*, Harmondsworth, Penguin Books (1955).

Crime and Delinquency

KLARE, H., *Anatomy of Prison*, London, Hutchinson (1960).

MACLURE, STUART (ed.), *Delinquency and Discipline*, Councils and Education Press (1962).

MAYS, J. B., *Growing Up In The City*, Liverpool University Press (1964).

—— *Crime and the Social Structure*, London, Faber (1967).

MORRIS, PAULINE, *Prisoners and Their Families*, London, Allen and Unwin (1965).

PARKER, TONY, *The Unknown Citizen*, Harmondsworth, Penguin Books (1966).

WEST, D. J., *The Young Offender*, London, Duckworth (1967).

Education

CRAFT, M., RAYNOR, J., COHEN, L. (eds.), *Linking Home and School*, London, Longmans (1967).

ELVIN, H. L., *Education and Contemporary Society*, London, Watts (1965).

H.M.S.O., *Half Our Future* (The Newsom Report), London (1963).

JACKSON, B., and MARSDEN, B., *Education and the Working Class*, London, Routledge and Kegan Paul (1962).

MAYS, J. B., *The School in its Social Setting*, London, Longmans (1967).

——, QUINE, W., and PICKETT, K., *School of Tomorrow*, London, Longmans (1968).

PEDLEY, R., *The Comprehensive School*, Harmondsworth, Penguin Books (1963).

The Family

DUNSTAN, G. R., *The Family Is Not Broken*, London, SCM Press (1962).

FLETCHER, R., *The Family and Marriage in Britain*, Harmondsworth, Penguin Books (1966).

MUSGROVE, F., *The Family, Education and Society*, London, Routledge and Kegan Paul (1966).

WYNN, M., *Fatherless Families*, London, Michael Joseph, (1964)

YOUNGHUSBAND, E. (ed.), *Social Work With Families*, London, Allen and Unwin (1965).

YUDKIN, S. and HOLME, A., *Working Mothers and Their Children*, London, Michael Joseph (1963).

Planning and Community

JACOBS, JANE, *The Death and Life of Great American Cities*, Harmondsworth, Penguin Books (1964).

JENNINGS, H., *Societies in the Making*, London, Routledge and Kegan Paul (1962).

KUENSTLER, P. (ed.), *Community Organisation in Great Britain*, London, Faber (1961).

MANN, P., *An Approach to Urban Sociology*, London, Routledge and Kegan Paul (1965).

MUMFORD, LEWIS, *The Culture of Cities*, London, Secker and Warburg (1938).

NICHOLSON, J. H., *New Communities in Britain*, London, National Council of Social Service (1961).

WILLMOTT, P. and YOUNG, M., *Family and Class in a London Suburb*, London, Routledge and Kegan Paul (1960).

YOUNG, M. and WILLMOTT, P., *Family and Kinship in East London*, London, Routledge and Kegan Paul (1957).

Youth

ABRAMS, M., *The Teenage Consumer*, London Press Exchange (Part I, 1959; Part 2, 1961).

CARTER, M., *Into Work*, Harmondsworth, Penguin Books (1966).

FYVEL, T. R., *The Insecure Offenders*, London, Chatto and Windus (1961).

JORDAN, G. W. and FISHER, E. M., *Self-Portrait of Youth*, London, Heinemann (1955).

LEECH, K. and JORDAN, B., *Drugs for Young People: Their Use and Misuse*, London, Religious Education Press (1967).

MACLURE, STUART (ed.), *Teenage Morals*, London, Councils and Education Press (1961).

MAYS, J. B., *The Young Pretenders*, London, Sphere Books (1968).

MORSE, M., *The Unattached*, Harmondsworth, Penguin Books (1965).

PATEY, E., *Young People Now*, London, SCM Press (1964).

SCHOFIELD, M., *The Sexual Behaviour of Young People*, London, Longmans (1965).

WILLMOTT, P., *Adolescent Boys in East London*, London, Routledge and Kegan Paul (1966).

WALL, W. D., *Child of Our Times*, London, National Children's Home and Orphanage (1959).

General

BERGER, PETER, *Invitation to Sociology*, Harmondsworth, Penguin Books (1966).

BOTTOMORE, T., *Sociology: A Guide to Problems and Literature*, London, Allen and Unwin (1962).

222

FORDER, A. (ed.), *The Social Services of Modern England*, London, Routledge and Kegan Paul (1968).

GABOR, DENNIS, *Inventing The Future*, Harmondsworth, Penguin Books (1964).

HALLORAN, J., *Control Or Consent*, London, Sheed and Ward (1963).

—— and BROTHERS (eds.), *Uses of Sociology*, London, Sheed and Ward (1965).

HALMOS, P., *The Faith of the Counsellors*, London, Constable (1965).

MACKENZIE, N., *A Guide to the Social Sciences*, London, Weidenfeld and Nicolson (1966).

MARSH, D., *The Future of the Welfare State*, Harmondsworth, Penguin Books (1964).

TITMUSS, R. M., *Essays on the Welfare State*, London, Allen and Unwin (1958).

YOUNG, M., *The Rise of the Meritocracy*, Harmondsworth, Penguin Books (1961).